OLD TESTAMENT

Bible Sketches for Children

Lillenas Drama

OLD TESTAMENT
Bible Sketches for Children

24 Interactive Scripts for Youth and Adults to Perform for Kids

by Gillette Elvgren

Theatre Arts, Regent University

RESOURCE *Publications* • Eugene, Oregon

Resource Publications
A division of Wipf and Stock Publishers
199 W 8th Ave, Suite 3
Eugene, OR 97401

Old Testament Sketches for Children
24 Interactive Scripts for Youth and Adults to Perform for Kids
By Elvgren, Gillette, Jr.
Copyright © 1997 by Elvgren, Gillette, Jr. All rights reserved.
Softcover ISBN-13: 978-1-6667-1198-1
Hardcover ISBN-13: 978-1-6667-1199-8
eBook ISBN-13: 978-1-6667-1200-1
Publication date 3/16/2021
Previously published by Lillenas Publishing Company, 1997

This edition is a scanned facsimile of the original edition published in 1997.

Contents

About the Author

Gillette Elvgren has been writing for over 20 years. His plays have been produced by professional theatre companies throughout the United States and Canada. He is cofounder and resident playwright for Saltworks Theatre Company in Pittsburgh, as well as being resident writer for Children's Ministries, Philadelphia. While a professor at the University of Pittsburgh, he was head of the MFA directing program and staff director for the Three Rivers Shakespeare Festival. Presently, he is in the departments of television and theatre arts at Regent University, Virginia Beach.

A catalog of other plays by Gillette Elvgren can be obtained by writing:

Gillette Elvgren
641 Aquila Dr.
Chesapeake, VA 23320
804-548-2071
gillelv@regent.edu

Playwright's Notes

The sketches found in this volume were originally created for Children's Sand and Surf Mission over a 25-year period and have been tried and tested on beaches all along the eastern seaboard, Texas, and California. CSSM is a high-powered evangelistic program for children ages 5 to 13 that has been in existence for over 130 years and that has devised an energetic, highly visual approach to telling children about Bible truths in England, Australia, Canada, and more recently, the United States. On these missions, nonprofessional teams come together for a two-week period, train for two days, and are launched into their programs. This gives you a clue as to how these dramas evolved as 8- to 10-minute sketches that can be organized with two one-hour rehearsals, easily memorized, very visual, and very energetic.

Since they first appeared on the beaches back in 1971, these plays have been produced in a number of other venues as well—in churches, Vacation Bible Schools, camps, inner-city missions, street theatre, and used as a general aid to Bible storytelling. Practical applications for these plays are described below. Remember, the nature of these plays is such that they can go any place and be produced by just about anybody.

WHO ARE THESE SKETCHES FOR? Though they are primarily directed toward children's audiences (ages 5 to 13), the comedy, fast-paced action, and eternal biblical truths elucidated make them generally appealing to the entire family. Youth audiences (ages 13 to 17) might find themselves a little inhibited about jumping in when the plays call for audience participation, but they love to watch the younger children become part of the action. These plays have been performed with success before church congregations, prison audiences, all kinds of summer camps, on television, in every imaginable Christian education environment, and in senior citizen homes.

WHO PERFORMS THESE SKETCHES? The plays were originally written to be performed for children by adults or teens. But over the last three decades just about every imaginable combination of different age-groups has been brought together to perform these sketches. These include amateur and professional drama companies; middle and high school children in schools and churches performing them for elementary age children and for their church congregations; mission teams overseas, on beaches, and in the inner city. It is not recommended that these dramas be performed exclusively by children under the age of 12, but child actors can be effectively mixed with adults and teens to form an effective intergenerational mix.

HOW CAN I USE THEM IN MY CHURCH? If you are thinking of starting up a drama ministry in your church or if you already have one, these sketches are designed to be nonthreatening, small-cast, low-budget, humorous teaching and entertainment vehicles that any drama group can mount with only two rehearsals. Specifically they have been used in the past as vehicles for a teen or adult drama team to take to the various Christian education classrooms on any given Sunday. This adds an exciting, visual, dramatic element to the classroom, stimulates discussion, and can be followed up with creative dramatic exercises in the classroom so that the children can reexperience the drama that they have just seen. They can be a substitute for the children's sermon or for the adult sermon in any church service.

HOW CAN I USE THEM AS DRAMA OUTREACH FROM MY CHURCH? Very quickly you will discover that the popularity of these dramas and the excitement they generate among your own congregation and among the different mix of acting age-groups that you have put together to mount them will result in a desire to share your product through other venues. Because they are short and uncomplicated they make excellent street dramas that can be performed in parks, playgrounds, and at children's rallies. They offer a variety to the traditional recreation and entertainment available for children at church retreats and as an ongoing event at Vacation Bible Schools. Some of the series (David, Daniel) exist as five dramas that can be done separately but also can be strung together as a series, thus making them perfect for a one-week (five-day) summer Bible school experience. You can also offer them to home school group meetings.

WHAT ABOUT THE CHRISTIAN SCHOOL THAT I AM INVOLVED IN? These plays serve as wonderful starter plays that have important teaching messages and a high theatrical quotient for drama clubs and scene work in drama class. The various series of plays can be presented as a continuing hour's entertainment for assemblies and for evening shows as well as drama competitions. Again, as in the churches, these are effective vehicles for the older children to perform for the younger, and to thereby develop some of the self-esteem through the audience recognition that is so important for the developing teen. It has been established that problem teens with drop-out potential can be turned around through the proactive involvement with a productive drama team. Drama increases the socialization factor through its necessary ensemble requirements, teaches discipline, and provides the troubled student with the very important self-esteem of having accomplished something meaningful.

HOW CAN THESE PLAYS HELP IN MY STORYTELLING? The art of telling stories from Scripture to children is, I believe, at the heart of Christian education. Drama is a form of storytelling enhanced by image and movement and interaction. Much can be culled from these sketches that can enrich your own storytelling techniques. Good storytelling involves playing other characters besides just an omniscient narrator. These plays will help you by providing dialogue sequences you can use, dramatic hooks you can transpose to grab the children's attention, special insights into the meanings of the stories, and fresh insights into character and action struggles and victories. Especially important will be an understanding that you will obtain in building a suspenseful dramatic structure for your story. Look carefully at the plays, and you can see how it is done—creating a context, establishing effective obstacles and antagonists, building to that dramatic climax.

REMEMBER: Have fun with these sketches. Just the fact that you have taken the time to prepare, memorize, and perform these dramas for the children in your church, your school, or your neighborhood will be appreciated. May your love for our Father, for these children, and for the excitement of performance shine through you as you give yourself to others through these plays.

Performing These Plays for Children

These plays are designed to be highly theatrical, visual, and full of physical action as well as humor. This tells you that energy and commitment to fast pacing, staying on top of dialogue cues, and not being slow on your exits and entrances are essential to capture the style of these plays for children. Below are listed some acting and staging notes that you should consider when rehearsing and performing these sketches for children.

PROPS

Bring all relevant props or facsimiles thereof to the rehearsal. A prop is any object that the actor can carry in his hand. Also, if an actor is going to use a cape or a hat or some costume piece that will have to be mastered, bring those along. Having props available even for the first rehearsal will help rather than hinder your actors and will provide them with the first sense of character and objectives. It will also give you a visual image of the action that will inspire your directing. Larger-than-life props; signs; fun, colorful, costume pieces are all part of the high-profile production style that should be a featured mark in any production of these sketches.

THE SET

It is recommended that you devise some sort of curtained area upstage where your actors can go behind in order to establish changes to costume, pick up needed props, and/or indicate changes in time and place. This can be as simple as stringing a curtain between two poles supported by heavy flag stands. A more elaborate plan would be to construct a self-standing curtained area made from PVC tubing and a polyester curtain so that it won't wrinkle. This is lightweight, can be easily broken down into small units, and can be set up in about 10 minutes.

You can mount these plays in a space as small as 12 feet by 12 feet. Play the dramas in front of your curtain, but use the curtain for entrances, exits, and for peeking through and around. In one production, Goliath was a huge rod puppet that appeared from behind the curtain and rose to a height of 12 feet. Scenes can be revealed by opening the curtain. Scenic cut-outs and signs like "Road to Jerusalem" can be hung in front of the curtains. Your possibilities are endless.

CHARACTERIZATION

Even though these sketches often have a cartoon feel about them, you should encourage the actors to explore who their characters are and what these characters want as fully as possible. If the performers begin to investigate the following questions about their characters, their characterizations will be more specific and fully realized.

WHAT DO YOU WANT? What is the character's objective. For example, Samuel wants to find the Lord's anointed—now! Your character's objective should be active, not past tense, and it should be something the actor can pursue onstage.

OBSTACLES: What is standing in the way of your character getting what he or she wants? In what active way does your character confront this obstacle? Delilah's objective is to discover what makes Samson so strong. The obstacle is that Samson prevaricates. So she must find individual and unique ways of getting around this and obtaining her objective. She pouts, comes onto him in an acceptable manner, gets a little angry, and so forth.

WHAT ARE THE GIVEN CIRCUMSTANCES? How old is your character? What physical traits does he or she have? Where has your character just been? Where is he or she going? What is the time, the temperature, the season, the environment, and so on? All of these questions might not be answered in the script, but you should go ahead and make them up for the portrayal of a fuller and richer character. Have your actors begin by exploring how the character might talk, walk, or breathe. What habits might he or she have? What are their likes and dislikes? For example, the hand-wringing worrier captured in Mordecai in the Esther series should be reflected in his slightly pleading, bent-over posture, the way he worriedly strokes his beard, rolls his eyes, and so on. Remember, these sketches are not heavy, realistic dramas, but rather quick-moving, often comic renditions of Bible stories. In addition, though the characters are based on biblical models, do not try to put on a period style of movement or voice. Often times, finding a contemporary equivalency best suits the intent of these plays. For example, David and his brothers can be played as American teenage types as can Meschach, Shadrach and Abednego. Broad, quick character strokes should be used so that characters can be quickly and comfortably identified. In "Daniel and the Lions," Advisers 1 and 2 are sly, opportunistic, but bumbling types not unlike the three stooges. At the same time, moments of emotional truth and revelation of character and action should be played with utmost reality. Thus, the moment that David confronts Goliath or Abraham stands over Isaac with a knife should not be satirized or exploited for comic potential. These scripts mix comedy and serious drama at the turn of a hat.

PERFORMANCE READY

The more you work together, the faster you will be able to get these plays up to performance quality. A couple of one-hour rehearsals should give you all the time you want if your director is prepared. And even this time can be cut down. Remember, you are not looking necessarily for a professional production. What you want is to communicate biblical truths in a fast-paced, energetic manner. Energy makes up for experience. A few hints on how to find and maintain this energy:

a. The director should exude energy and should set the model for the kind of drive needed to bring these sketches off effectively.

b. Never have periods of time when some actor is not onstage.

c. Pick up cues. Don't let there be a gap between lines unless it is fully acted out. Remember: acting is reacting.

d. Don't let the delivery of lines be too slow. Keep the internal pacing going.

e. If you are in sight of the audience, keep acting.

And above all have fun! Your witness as a group of Christian adults throwing yourselves into the wild, exuberant energy of these sketches will communicate to children that you are doing something special for them and that this Christian faith of ours is an exciting, moving, and wonderful adventure.

THE STORY
OF THE CREATION

(Company enters.)

NARRATOR: In the play we're doing for you today, we play bad guys.

(They act out this as well as various other people, animals, plants, etc.)

And we play good guys. We play animals. And we play flowers and trees.

(All the actors except one become trees and flowers.)

I said we play flowers and trees.

(Actor playing monkey still plays monkey. NARRATOR whispers in his ear. He turns into a tree.)

Can you guess what I told that monkey, to turn him [her] into a tree? Well, what is a monkey's favorite food? Bananas! That's right! I told him he could be a banana tree. And now for our play.

This morning we are going to tell you how God made all of creation: how He made the stars and how He made us.

Creation Song
God made the stars in the sky.
God made the heaven on high.
God made the earth and the ocean and the seas.
God made the flowers and the itty bitty bees.
God made everything you see.
God made everything for me.
God made everything, everything new.
God made me, and God made you.

NARRATOR: Yes, God made me, and God made you. In the beginning, God made the heaven and the earth. He made the entire universe and all the stars.

(Two actors enter carrying stars on sticks.)

STARS: Twinkle, twinkle little stars . . .

NARRATOR: Please, no more songs. And He made the sun.

SUN *(has large cutout hat):* Don't touch me. I'm hot.

NARRATOR: Yes, she's a sizzler all right. And He made the moon.

MOON: I'm the moon, and contrary to popular opinion, I am not made from green cheese.

2ND MOON: Neither am I.

NARRATOR: Wait a minute. Something's wrong here. God made the stars. (STARS *twinkle and start to sing.* NARRATOR *quiets them.*) And God made the sun. (*The* SUN *sizzles.*) And God made the moon.

MOONS: Right here. Right here.

NARRATOR: Maybe you kids can tell me what's wrong? (*Response from children*) That's right. He made only one moon. Scram, moon. (*One* MOON *exits.*) And on the earth, He made all kinds of plants. Will you kids help us in becoming plants? While we sing the creation song, I want you over here to be beautiful flowers, and I want you over here to be tall, strong trees, and I want you over here to be thorn bushes with lots of prickles. Presto, and God made the plants. Let's see all of these plants come to bloom. Good, very good. And then God made the animals. (*All the company make exotic animal noises.*) And then God made man. (ADAM *enters.*) Man was made in God's image. He was a glorious creature. He could run. (ADAM *runs.*) He could jump. (ADAM *jumps.*) He could even leap this pile of sand in a single bound. (ADAM *leaps and falls.*) And he was a lot smarter than the other animals.

ADAM: Two plus two is . . . is . . . (*Response from audience*) . . . four. That's right, just checking to see if you are on your toes. What's four plus four, divided by four, and then multiplied by four? (*Response*) Eight is right. Sharp bunch of kids. Oh that's right. I forgot. I'm Adam, the first man on earth, none of you even exist yet.

(*He goes to get animals.*)

NARRATOR: One of Adam's main duties was to name the animals. Here come some animals. Let's see how well he does and if you can help him out.
(*Dog enters barking. Adam guesses, "Hippopotamus." Audience corrects him. Monkey enters screeching. Adam guesses, "Platypus." Audience corrects him . . . and so forth.*)
But I want you all to know, that once Adam got his names straight, he never forgot them. And then into this garden, God brought Adam a very special someone. Who was that? (*Response*) You're right. It was Eve.

EVE: Hi, Adam. Ooh, you're kind of cute.

ADAM: Awwww. You're kind of cute yourself, Eve.

EVE: Let's go romp with the animals, Adam.

ADAM: Awwww.

(*She drags him off.*)

NARRATOR: And also into this garden, God put a beautiful fruit tree: the tree of knowledge of good and evil. (TREE *enters.*) God forbade both Adam and Eve to eat the fruit because then they would know evil in having disobeyed God and they would be separated from Him because of their sin.

(EVE *enters and is being chased by* ADAM. *She hides behind the* TREE, *which is an actor holding a few pieces of forbidden fruit in hand.* EVE *eludes* ADAM *who runs off.*)

EVE: Oh, that fruit looks so good. It wouldn't be too bad if I just had one bite. I'm so thirsty. What do you kids think? Should I have a bite? (*Response from audience*) You're right. Better leave it alone.

(SNAKE, *played by an actor or a puppet sock, appears. Be sure* SNAKE *hisses all the Ss.*)

SNAKE: Did God forbid you to eat the fruit of the trees of the garden, my pretty lady?

EVE: Oh, you startled me. God said that we may eat the fruit of the trees of the garden except the tree that is in the middle of the garden. He said that if we touched this fruit or ate it, we would die. Now, I don't exactly know what this dying means, but from the way He said it, I don't think it would be a happy thing.

SNAKE: Fiddlesticks! You will not die. God knows that the day you eat of the fruit, your eyes shall be opened and you will be like gods, knowing good from evil. Don't you want to be like God, to know what He knows?

EVE: I guess so. What do you think? (*Response, no, from audience*) Well, I'll try it anyway. (*Takes a bite*) Oh dear, what have I done!

(ADAM *runs on. He sees what has happened.*)

ADAM: Uh, oh! (*Debates if he should eat and be with* EVE, *or should he abandon her. She holds the fruit out to him. Reluctantly, he eats it.*) Excuse me, Eve, but I have to put some clothes on.

(*They run to put towels around themselves.*)

EVE: Yes, it is getting chilly.

GOD'S VOICE: Adam, where are you?

ADAM: I am afraid, and I have hidden myself.

GOD'S VOICE: Have you eaten the fruit of the tree from which I commanded you not to eat?

ADAM: She did it, Lord. She gave me the fruit to eat.

GOD'S VOICE: What is this you have done?

EVE: Er . . . I . . . it was the serpent who tempted me. (*Lamely*) And I ate.

GOD'S VOICE: Now you shall know death. You, Adam, will have to plow the rough ground to make a living through the sweat of your brow, and you, Eve, will know great pain when you bear children. And for disobeying me, you will be driven from this Garden of Eden. (ADAM *and* EVE, *looking very unhappy, leave.*) And for you, serpent, you will be condemned to slither in the dust all your days.

17

(SNAKE, *who has been trying to sneak off, falls to the ground and slithers his exit.*)

NARRATOR: Adam and Eve sinned, and they were separated from God. From that time forth, all people have known death and all people are separated from God from the time they are born. If all of us were separated from God because of sin from the time we were born, is there any way that we can get back with God? Yes, for God sent His only Son, Jesus Christ, to die for our sins. And He died on the Cross that you and I would have life forever with the Father. That's good news!

THE END

NOAH AND THE FLOOD

(Company enters.)

NARRATOR: Today, let's see if you kids can guess what story we are going to do for you. We'll give you come clues, and you tell us what Bible story we will play for you.

(Company acts out following.)

ACTOR 1: It has lots of bad guys.

ACTOR 2: It has one real good guy.

ACTOR 3: It has God.

ACTOR 4: It has lots of water.

ACTOR 5: It has a boat.

ACTOR 6: It has all kinds of animals.

(Kids should have guessed correctly by now.)

NARRATOR: That's right, this is the story of Noah and the Flood. Let's sing the "Noah Song" now.

NOAH SONG
The Lord looked down from heaven.
He didn't like what He saw.
The Lord looked down from heaven
At the people breaking the law.
The people were bad, and the Lord got mad,
He sent the rain, rain, rain
On the shame, shame, shame below,
Woe, woe, woe.
The Lord looked down from heaven.
He didn't like what He saw.
The Lord looked down from heaven
At the people breaking the law.
But Noah He spared 'cause for Noah He cared,
He sent the rain, rain, rain
On the shame, shame, shame below,
Woe, woe, woe.

NARRATOR: Yes, the Lord did look down from heaven; and everywhere He looked, people were wicked and sinful. It broke His heart, and He was sorry that He had made them. When He looked to the left, what do you think He saw? He saw people who fought with each other.

SINNER 1: I don't like your nose; take that.

SINNER 2: I don't like your hair; take that.

(They exit fighting.)

NARRATOR: He looked to the right and saw people who lied.

SINNER 3 *(to audience):* I can swallow the ocean there in one swallow. Cross my heart. Do you believe me?

NARRATOR: And He looked and saw people who loved money more than anything.

SINNER 4: I love money. I love the feel of money. I love the smell of money. *(Eating)* Why I even love the taste of money.

NARRATOR: And He looked down and saw people who even loved themselves more than anything.

SINNER 5: Hi, ya'll. Aren't I beautiful? I just love myself. Which of you darling little children would like a big ruby red kiss from me? Oh, well, bye-bye.

(She exits mumbling, "Oh, you little darling" and kissing herself.)

NARRATOR: Well, you can imagine how all this made God feel. He was going to send a flood which would kill all people and all animals. But wait, couldn't God find at least one man who was good? *(Response from audience)* Right, He looked down and found Noah (NOAH *enters.)* Noah was a pleasure to the Lord. He worked hard. He hardly ever sinned.

(SINNERS 1 AND 2 enter fighting. SINNER 5 follows them kissing herself.)

SINNERS 1 AND 2: Put up your dukes, Noah. Wanna fight?

NOAH: No, thank you.

SINNER 5: How about one of my ruby red kisses?

NOAH: No, thank you.

SINNER 4: How about some delicious money, Noah?

NOAH: No, thank you.

SINNER 3: Well, what do you do for fun anyway?

NOAH: I praise the Lord and do a lot of praying too.

SINNER 4: Well, I'm going to count my money.

SINNER 1: I'm going to pick a fight.

SINNER 2: Yeah, me too.

SINNER 5: And I'm going to go find myself a mirror and look at my beautiful self. Oh, I love you.

(Exits kissing herself)

NARRATOR: And God told Noah that He was going to send a flood, but the Lord said He would watch over Noah and his family. So He told Noah to build a boat—a big boat for himself, his family, and all kinds of animals.

SINNER 3: My, would you look at that. What are you doing, Noah?

NOAH: I'm building a boat, an ark.

SINNERS *(mocking disbelief)*: An ark?

NOAH: There's going to be a flood that covers all the land.

SINNERS: A flood?

NOAH: The Lord told me.

SINNERS: The Lord? You must be crazy!

NOAH *(putting his hand out)*: I think it's going to begin raining. *(Brings out his umbrella)* Yup, I just felt a drop.

NARRATOR: And it began to rain. Noah went into the boat with his family. Then came the animals two-by-two. What kind of animals are these? And the rain came down harder and harder. Wait, I don't feel any rain. *(To audience)* Could you make some thunder noises? *(Response)* That's good. I still don't feel any rain. Could you make some more thunder noises? *(Response)* And now some wind. *(Response)* Very good. I'll go see how the boat is doing.
  (A boat can be made in the following manner: Using four actors who have joined hands fore and aft to make the bow and stern of the boat. In the middle have Noah on the shoulders of another actor. Actors do the following actions.)
  And just as God had promised, after 40 days, the rain stopped. And Noah sent out a dove to see if he could return with a green branch, and then he would know if there was any land in sight. But the dove could find no place to land and came back with nothing. A little later, Noah sent the dove out again, and this time it returned with an olive branch in its beak so that Noah knew dry land was near.

NOAH: Land ahoy. *(The ship lands.)* Come on all you animals! Stick together now. You've got to populate the world, so start having babies. Thank You, Lord, for bringing us through safe and sound. I praise You, Lord. Praise the Lord!

NARRATOR: And everyone—animals and Noah's family—praised the Lord.

EVERYONE: Praise the Lord!

(They dance in a circle and exit singing the "Noah Song" under the following speech.)

NARRATOR: And because Noah had done what God wanted, God promised never to send another flood against His people. Remember, Noah obeyed his Lord. Because of this, he was saved from God's anger. God has promised each one of us the very same salvation. If you love your Lord Jesus Christ and obey and make Him King of your life, you will also be saved. And that's wonderful.

THE END

ABRAHAM AND ISAAC

Bible Verse: But God demonstrated His own love toward us, in that while we were yet sinners, Christ died for us *(Romans 5:8).*

(ABRAHAM *enters.)*

ABRAHAM: Howdy, kids, my name is Abraham, and this story is about me. I lived a long time ago. Why, I even lived before Moses, bless his soul. I have traveled through many lands and many cities, wherever the good Lord has sent me. But I know the Lord loves me because He has seen me through many a hard day. But do you know what I want more than anything else? I want a son. *(Kneels)*

   O Lord, Jehovah, what good are all Your blessings when I have no son? Some other member of my household will inherit the wealth You have given me.

(CHORUS *enters and sings.)*

CHORUS: Abraham, oh Abraham,
                  He wants a son so bad;
               Abraham, oh Abraham,
                  He wants a good strong lad.

ABRAHAM: So I called to the Lord way up high,
               I called to the Lord way up in the sky,
               I said, "Lord, You know I have no one,
               So why don't You send me a healthy son?"

(Chorus: sung by NARRATOR *and two helpers.)*

ABRAHAM: And the Lord said, "Don't you worry Abe.
               I love you, and I'll send a babe.
               He'll be happy, and he'll be strong.
               And you won't have to wait too terribly long."

(Chorus)

ABRAHAM: And when I heard that, I leapt with joy;
               For the Lord was going to send me a boy;
               And I praised the almighty, wonderful Lord
               For promising me this reward.

(Chorus)

ABRAHAM: But do you know how long the Lord made me wait? The Lord told me when I was 99 that I would have a son; and that Sarah, my wife, who was almost as old as I, was going to bear that child. Here comes Sarah now.

(SARAH *enters moving like an old lady.*)

SARAH: Howdy, Abe.

ABRAHAM: Howdy, Sarah. How're ya feeling?

SARAH: Oh, I'm not complainin'.

ABRAHAM: How's the toe?

SARAH: A bit slow.

ABRAHAM: How's the back?

SARAH: A bit slack.

ABRAHAM: The Lord said we were going to have a son.

SARAH *(laughing):* That's a funny one.

ABRAHAM: Well, I didn't want to hurt the Lord's feelings, so I turned away from Him and had myself a good laugh.

SARAH: Me, have a baby? Impossible, I'm too old. I'm 90 years old, going on 100. These old bones won't do what they used to do. Why that's one of the funniest things I ever heard.

(*While they are laughing, one of the cast brings a bundle to* SARAH.)

ABRAHAM: Look, Sarah, a gift from the Lord. *(To audience)* And do you know what God called this little baby? He called him "Isaac." Do you know what "Isaac" means? It means "laughter." The Lord called the boy "Isaac" or "laughter" because Sarah and I did so much laughing.

SARAH: Isn't he cute?

ABRAHAM: He looks just like you.

SARAH: No, he doesn't. He looks just like you.

ABRAHAM: He has your toes.

SARAH: He has your nose.

ABRAHAM AND SARAH: Isn't the Lord wonderful?

(ISAAC *comes onstage.*)

ABRAHAM: And Isaac grew to be a handsome, young boy, and the Lord promised that he would be a source of blessing for all the nations of the earth.

CHORUS: Abraham, oh Abraham
                    Now he has his son
                 Abraham, oh Abraham
                    And a son is a lot of fun.

ABRAHAM: Isaac likes to run all day,
                 Through the months of April and May,
                 He likes to jump and hop and play,
                 In that glorious month of May.

(Chorus)

ABRAHAM: But you know who Isaac loved best of all?
                 Even more than playing ball?
                 He loved his God with all his might
                 'Cause in his heart, he knew that was right.
              But one day, God tested my faith.

GOD'S VOICE: Abraham!

ABRAHAM: Yes, Lord!

GOD'S VOICE: Take your only son, Isaac, whom you love so much; and sacrifice him as a burnt offering upon one of the mountains.

ABRAHAM: My son, Lord? My only son?

GOD'S VOICE: Your son, Abraham.

ABRAHAM: The next morning, I chopped some wood for the offering. (ABRAHAM *and* ISAAC *mime chopping wood.*) And then we traveled for three days, carrying the wood, and went to the mountain.
        (CHORUS *sings a mournful chorus to* "Abraham's Song.")
        And when we got to the mountain, I prepared the altar where I was going to sacrifice my son.

ISAAC: Father, we have the wood and the matches to light the fire, but where is the lamb for the sacrifice?

ABRAHAM: God will see to it, Son. Kneel down.

(He ties ISAAC's *hands.)*

ISAAC: Father, are you going to sacrifice me to the Lord?

ABRAHAM: Yes, Son. It is what the Lord has commanded. Are you ready, my Son?

ISAAC: Yes, Father.

(The knife is raised.)

GOD'S VOICE: Abraham. Lay down your knife. Don't hurt the lad in any way, for I know that I am first in your life. You have not withheld even your beloved son from Me.

ABRAHAM AND ISAAC *(together):* Praise the Lord!

CHORUS: Abraham, oh Abraham,
                  Now he has his son;
                  Abraham, oh Abraham,
                  And a son is a lot of fun.

ABRAHAM: My faith in You is always restored.
                  How I love You, love You, Lord;
                  I will always follow Your lead,
                  For You have given me all I need.

(Chorus)

ABRAHAM: And now you've seen how the Lord loved me and spared my son. But let me ask you a question. Did God spare His Son, Jesus, from dying on the Cross? No, He didn't. He loves us so much, that He gave His only Son so that those of us who really believe in Jesus might have eternal life. And that's somethin' special.

THE END

JOSEPH AND HIS BROTHERS: PART I

Bible Verse: And God Himself has said that one must love not only God, but his brother too *(1 John 4:21, TLB)*.

NARRATOR: This is the story of Joseph and his brothers.

JOSEPH WAS A DREAMER

CAST: Joseph was a dreamer, Joseph was a dreamer;
             And he loved his Lord on high.
        Joseph was a dreamer, Joseph was a dreamer;
             And his love was something money can't buy.
        Joseph was a dreamer, Joseph was a dreamer;
             And in his heart he knew—
        Joseph was a dreamer, Joseph was a dreamer—
             That you should love your brother too.

NARRATOR: Yes, this is the Bible story of Joseph and his brothers. And just like the song said, Joseph was a dreamer. How many of you kids have ever had dreams?

(Response from audience)

BROTHER 1: I dreamed about snakes last night.

NARRATOR: I'll bet it gave you a terrible fright.

BROTHER 1: I can't remember much, try as I might.

NARRATOR *(to audience)*: Let's help him remember his dream. Become snakes with me. Can your arms become crawly, slithery snakes?

(Audience participates and BROTHER 1 is frightened and runs off.)

BROTHER 2: I dreamed I was flying high over ocean and sand.

NARRATOR: But how did you ever take off from the land?

BROTHER 2: Uh, I don't remember. I did something with my arms I think.

NARRATOR *(to audience)*: Can you kids guess what she [he] did with her arms to take off? Let's flap with our arms and help her remember. *(Kids participate.)*

BROTHER 2: That's it! I'm flying, I'm flying. Oh, but I'm afraid of heights. *(Flies off and crashes)*

NARRATOR: But when Joseph dreamed, he remembered his dreams because his dreams came from the Lord. Yes, the Lord talked to Joseph through his dreams when he slept at night.

(JOSEPH *runs on.*)

JOSEPH: Father Jacob! Father Jacob! The Lord has given me another dream, and this one was in Technicolor.

(JACOB *can be played by* NARRATOR, *who puts on hat or beard and staff.*)

JACOB: Oh, another dream? The Lord has certainly blessed me by giving me such a son in my old age. Here, take this beautiful robe, Joseph, because I love you so. And tell us the dream when your brothers get back. *(To audience)* Do you know how many brothers Joseph had? Not one . . . not seven . . . but ten. And all of them hated Joseph for being my favorite son.

(*Three brothers enter—male or female, it doesn't matter. These three will play all the brothers by making fast costume and hat changes. For example: one brother could wear a towel around his middle. As he plays another brother, he could wrap the towel around his shoulders, and for another he could wrap it around his head. Some could be tall, short, or fat, etc. This should be almost like a vaudeville routine. Practice it because it will be used over and over.*)

BROTHER 1: I'm Reuben.

BROTHER 2: I'm Simeon.

BROTHER 3: And I'm Issachar.

BROTHER 1: I'm Judah.

BROTHER 2: I'm Levi.

BROTHER 3: And I'm Zebulun.

BROTHER 1: I'm Gad.

BROTHER 2: I'm Dan.

BROTHER 3: And I'm Naphtali.

BROTHER 1: I'm Asher.

BROTHER 2: And I'm Dasher and Prancer and Vixen.

(BROTHERS 1 AND 3 *hit* BROTHER 2 *on the head in comic style.*)

BROTHER 1: Oh, that Joseph, I hate him.

BROTHERS 2 AND 3: Yeah!

BROTHER 1: Him and his dreams—somebody ought to turn him off.

BROTHERS 2 AND 3: Yeah!

BROTHER 1: How come Father Jacob doesn't give us some new robes?

BROTHERS 2 AND 3: Yeah!

(JOSEPH *enters.*)

JOSEPH: Howdy, brothers! (Brothers 1, 2, *and* 3 *grumble.*) Let me tell you about my Technicolor dream. *(They grumble louder.)* We were in the field tying up sheaves of wheat. My sheaf stood up, and your sheaves all bowed before it.

(This could be done by having cardboard cutouts in background, or by drawing on chalkboard.)

BROTHER 2: Oh? So we bowed down to you did we? Who do you think you are, our king or something?

(BROTHERS *shake their fists and start toward* JOSEPH.)

JOSEPH: Wait! That's not all. I had another dream. This one was in Technicolor and Cinemascope. I dreamed the sun, the moon, and 11 stars bowed low before me.

(Cutouts appear and do action.)

BROTHER 3: Eleven stars stand for 11 brothers. Umph! We'll never bow down to you, Joseph.

BROTHERS: Never! *(ad lib)*

(BROTHERS *start after* JOSEPH.)

JOSEPH: Wait a minute. *(Nervously)* After all, it was just a dream. (BROTHERS *grumble off.)*

BROTHER 1: Let's go tend our sheep.

BROTHER 2: Yeah, sheep don't dream.

(JACOB *enters.)*

JACOB: Joseph, Joseph, come here.

JOSEPH: You called, Father?

JACOB: I'm a bit worried about your brothers. They are over in Shechem grazing the flocks. I want you to go and see how they are getting along.

JOSEPH: Whatever you say.

JACOB: Oh, by the way, when you are out there, keep your dreams to yourself—eh. Joseph, you know . . .

JOSEPH: Yes, I know. Good-bye, Father.

(He exits. BROTHERS *enter.)*

BROTHER 1: Look, here comes Mr. Dreamer, himself.

BROTHER 2: He has nerve coming out here.

BROTHER 3: I'll bet he's come to spy on us.

BROTHER 1: Let's finish him off for good. We'll kill him and throw him down that well.

ALL: Yeah!

*(*JOSEPH *enters.* BROTHERS *circle him.)*

BROTHER 1: Hello, Joseph.

BROTHER 2: Fancy meeting you here, Joseph.

BROTHER 3: What a nice robe you have, Joseph.

BROTHERS: Get him!

(They struggle. Knives are raised.)

BROTHER 1: Wait! Don't kill him. We don't want his blood on our hands. Throw him down the well alive. We'll sell him to a slave trader, make some money, and see our brother taken to another country as a slave. Get his coat.

(They take his coat and throw him down the well. BROTHERS *look down well.)*

ALL: Sweet dreams, Joseph. In Egypt!

(They exit. JACOB *enters.)*

JACOB: Joseph . . . Joseph . . . dead. Oh, woe is me.

*(*BROTHERS *enter piously.)*

BROTHERS: Yes, Father, here is his coat. Look at the blood. A lion must have eaten dear brother Joseph for lunch.

BROTHERS 1 AND 3: That's our hunch.

JACOB: Oh, I will die from sadness over the loss of my son.

(He exits weeping. BROTHERS *snicker and follow.)*

NARRATOR: And Joseph was sold into slavery and taken to Egypt. Will Joseph blame God for his misfortune?

*(*JOSEPH *enters in chains.)*

JOSEPH: Oh, thank You, Lord, for sparing my life. I'm a slave, but all things work for good for those who love You, O Lord. I don't know what will happen to me, but as long as I continue to trust in You, Lord, I won't be afraid. *(Exits)*

NARRATOR: And as long as each one of you trusts in Jesus, there is nothing that can happen to you that God cannot work for your good. Yes, things look pretty dark for Joseph. What will happen to him now? All alone, a slave in a foreign country, no family or friends. How will his dream come true? How will his brothers bow down to him now? Be sure to come back for the second exciting episode of Joseph and His Brothers.

END PART I

JOSEPH AND HIS BROTHERS: PART II

(NARRATOR *enters with* CHORUS.)

NARRATOR: And now it's time for the second part of the story of Joseph and His Brothers. Let's all sing the Joseph song. *(They sing "Joseph Was a Dreamer.")* If you remember yesterday, we left Joseph on his way to be sold as a slave in Egypt. His brothers, resenting the favor Joseph had with his father, Jacob, and with the Lord, threw him down a well and took his robe. Then they splattered it with sheep's blood and showed it to Jacob, who wept bitterly at the loss of his son. And now we go to Egypt to see how Joseph is adapting to life as a slave.

(POTIPHAR *enters. Speaks to audience.*)

POTIPHAR: I'm Potiphar the mighty. I'm captain of the king's bodyguard. I'm also chief executioner, which means that if any of you kids get out of line . . . *(Draws his finger across his neck)* That's right, it's the end for you. I also own a big house, two swimming pools, and three chariots; so I need lots of slaves. Bring out that new batch of slaves. *(Three* SLAVES *are brought out.* JOSEPH *is the last.)*
  No, this one has a wart on his nose. Reject! Phew, this one has bad breath. Reject! *(Walks around* JOSEPH*)* Nice biceps. Good posture. He'll do. Accept.

(SLAVES *exit.*)

JOSEPH: You know, being a slave wasn't as bad as I thought it might be, for the Lord greatly blessed me and soon I became the top slave in Potiphar's household.

(POTIPHAR'S WIFE *enters and begins feeding* POTIPHAR *grapes.* SERVANTS 1, 2, *and 3 enter.*)

SERVANT 1: Master, Master, the well's run dry. What should we do?

POTIPHAR: Don't ask me, ask Joseph.

(SERVANT 1 *runs to* JOSEPH, *who gives instructions.*)

SERVANT 2: Master, Master, the silk has arrived by camel from India. How much should we buy?

POTIPHAR: Joseph takes care of those things. Now leave us alone.

SERVANT 3: Master, Master, would you like lamb or chicken for dinner tonight?

POTIPHAR: Lamb's fine, but check first with Joseph.

WIFE: Joseph this, Joseph that . . . my, but that new slave of yours certainly is handsome. Hey Potty, I think I just heard the king calling for you.

POTIPHAR: Oh bother, duty calls. Joseph, take care of things while I'm gone.

JOSEPH: Yes, Master.

(POTIPHAR *exits.*)

WIFE: Hi ya, handsome.

JOSEPH *(looking around):* Are you talking to me?

WIFE: You know, Joseph, you do such a good job of taking care of my husband's household and business affairs; how about taking care of me with a little kiss?

JOSEPH: My master trusts me with everything in the household. I can't betray him. It would be a great sin against God.

WIFE: But just one little ol' kiss . . . nobody's looking.

JOSEPH: God's looking.

WIFE: Who cares, a couple of kisses from me and . . .

JOSEPH: That's enough. I really have to be going.

(*They struggle.* JOSEPH *escapes, leaving his robe behind.*)

WIFE: Why that impudent slave. He ran away from me. So my kisses aren't good enough for him. But I've got his robe. I'll teach him to run away from me. Help! Help!

(POTIPHAR *enters.*)

POTIPHAR: I'm here, wife. What's wrong? Stop yelling!

WIFE: It's that slave of yours, Joseph. He attacked me. My screams scared him off, but here's his robe to prove it.

POTIPHAR: What? I never would have believed it of him. Umph! Arrest the slave and throw him into the dungeon.

(*A mad chase ensues.* JOSEPH *is captured and thrown into jail in chains.* POTIPHAR *and* WIFE *exit.* CUPBEARER *and* CHIEF BAKER *enter in chains.*)

CUPBEARER AND CHIEF BAKER: Oh, woe is us.

JOSEPH: Come now, life in jail can't be that bad.

CUPBEARER: I'm the official cupbearer. I carry the king's favorite cup. But the king got mad at me, and now my number's up.

CHIEF BAKER: I'm the official chief baker for the king. I bake his bread. I should be making cookies, but I'm here instead.

JOSEPH: Cheer up. Let's get a good night's sleep, and everything will look better in the morning.
(They sleep standing up. It is evident that the CUPBEARER *and* CHIEF BAKER *are having nightmares. They all awake.)*
You were both dreaming.

CUPBEARER: But what does the dream mean?

JOSEPH: Only God knows. Tell it to me, and God may tell me the answer.

CUPBEARER: I dreamed that there was a vine before me and that it had three branches with blossoms and lots of ripe juicy grapes . . . yum. I took the grapes and squeezed them into Pharaoh's cup and put the cup in his hand.

JOSEPH: The Lord has told me what the dream means. The three branches are three days. Within three days, the king of Egypt will take you from the jail, and once more you will serve him.

CUPBEARER: Yippee . . .

JOSEPH: Would you do me a favor? When you see the king, tell him what I have done for you. I was kidnapped and brought to Egypt and thrown into jail for doing nothing wrong.

CUPBEARER: Don't you worry, Joseph. I'll put in a good word for you . . . as soon as I get out. I won't forget.

BAKER: Now tell me what mine means. I dreamed that I had three baskets on my head, filled with bread. Then the birds came and began to pick at the bread from the top basket. Well? *(JOSEPH is silent.)* Bad news, eh?

JOSEPH: The three baskets stand for three days. In three days, the king will see you. The birds pecking mean that you will loose your head.

BAKER: Gulp!

(They exit. A runner comes on with sign "3 Days Later." PHARAOH enters.)

PHARAOH: I am Pharaoh, king of all Egypt. Bring me the cupbearer and the baker from the dungeon. *(They are thrown in.)* Cupbearer, here's my cup. Start bearing again.

CUPBEARER *(taking cup):* Yippee.

PHARAOH: And him . . . *(points to* BAKER*)* Off with his head.

(BAKER exits.)

CUPBEARER: Oh, by the way, King, I have something very important to tell you.

PHARAOH: Yes, hurry up. I don't have all day. What do you want?

CUPBEARER: I forgot. Never mind. Here, have another drink.

(They exit.)

NARRATOR: And Joseph stayed in jail. He stayed not days, not weeks, but years. Do you think he was mad? Do you think he planned to get revenge on Potiphar's wife for the trick she played on him? Here he comes now.

(JOSEPH enters.)

JOSEPH: Praise the Lord. I've been in jail two years now. O Lord, You have blessed me and made me the chief keeper of the jail. I don't know how long I will stay here, but I remain faithful to You because I know You have a good plan for my life.

NARRATOR: Do you praise the Lord and put your faith in God even when the going gets tough? That is when it really counts. Jesus never complained. Let me tell you, Jesus was always willing to follow God's plan, even though it meant being crucified and dying so that you and I could be put right with God. And now kids, come back next time to find out what happens to our prisoner behind bars in the third episode of Joseph and His Brothers.

END PART II

JOSEPH AND HIS BROTHERS: PART III

(CHORUS *enters, sings Joseph song.*)

NARRATOR: If you remember, Joseph had been sold into slavery in Egypt by his brothers, who were jealous of his being their father's favorite. In Egypt, Joseph had been thrown in jail for something he didn't do. And that's where we find him now—two years later.

(*Enter* JOSEPH *and two* SLAVES *in chains.* SLAVES *are singing dirgelike.*)

SLAVES: Sittin' in jail all day long,
Sittin' in jail, where we don't belong.
Sittin' in jail, where the food is bad.
Sittin' in jail, where we are tired and sad.
Listen to us shout.
Come and get us out.
Sittin' in jail all day long.

JOSEPH *(laughing):* Hey, don't look so glum. Life with the Lord can be fun anywhere.

SLAVE 1: Why don't you go someplace and have a nice long dream.

SLAVE 2: Yeah, and make it a nightmare.

(SLAVES *exit singing dirge.* JOSEPH *follows.*)

NARRATOR: Meanwhile in the palace, Pharaoh, the king, was having his own dreams.

(PHARAOH, CUPBEARER, *and* MAGICIANS *enter.*)

PHARAOH: Dreams, dreams, my kingdom for one night without any dreams. Some people dream about lollipops, and others dream about big rock candy pyramids. I dream about cows—yuck. I can't stand cows. Can't anybody tell me what my dream means?

CUPBEARER: Here are your magicians, Sire. Tell them the dream so that they can interpret it.

MAGICIAN 1: Ugga bugga, puddin' and pie. I see lollipops in the sky.

MAGICIAN 2: Violets are red, roses are blue, snakes go "hiss," and cows go "moo."

MAGICIANS: Tell us your dreams.

(The dreams are depicted with cardboard cutouts.)

PHARAOH: In my dream I was standing on the bank of the Nile, and seven cows, fat and sleek, came up out of the river and began to feed on the grass. Then just when everything seemed fine, out of the river came seven other cows; but these cows were so skinny their bones stuck out, and they had a terrible hungry look to their eyes. And do you know what they did?

MAGICIANS: No, what?

PHARAOH *(terrified):* The skinny cows ate the fat cows all up, right down to their hooves. And do you know what else?

MAGICIANS: No, what?

PHARAOH: The skinny cows didn't get any fatter; they stayed skinny.

MAGICIANS: Oh!

PHARAOH: Well, what does it mean?

MAGICIAN 1: It means . . . you are not supposed to eat hamburgers for seven years.

PHARAOH: Bah. Throw him in the dungeon for seven years. Now, what have you to say?

MAGICIAN 2: Gulp . . . The dream means . . . beware of going swimming in the Nile with skinny, hungry cows.

PHARAOH: Bah. Throw him in the Nile—with no life jacket. Can't anybody tell me what this dream means?

Cupbearer: Sire, I know someone who can tell you what your dream means. His name is . . . his name is . . . I've forgotten. Could you kids help? I've forgotten his name. *(They respond.)* Joseph! That's it. Thanks. He's in the dungeon.

PHARAOH: Bring him here at once.

(PHARAOH *snaps fingers.* JOSEPH *runs on.)*

PHARAOH: So you are Joseph. Let's see if you can tell me what the dream means. In my dream, I was standing on the bank of the Nile; and seven cows, fat and sleek, came up out of the river and began to feed on the grass. Then just when everything seemed fine, out of the river came seven other cows; but these cows were so skinny their bones stuck out, and they had a terrible hungry look to their eyes. Then the skinny cows ate the fat cows all up, and they didn't get any fatter.

JOSEPH: I don't know what the dream means, but my Lord does. *(Prays, receives answer)* The seven fat cows stand for seven years of plenty in the land of

Egypt. You will have all the food you need and lots left over. The seven skinny cows stand for seven lean years that will follow. During these years, the land will bring forth no food. People will starve. It will be a terrible time.

PHARAOH: Oh dear, what should I do?

JOSEPH: Pharaoh should select a wise man to be in charge of gathering in one fifth of the food during the seven years of plenty and storing it up for the seven years of famine.

PHARAOH: And you shall be that man.

JOSEPH: Praise the Lord and store the wheat.

NARRATOR: And the Lord made Joseph, a foreigner, a slave, and a prisoner, into the second most powerful man in Egypt. The Lord is great and mighty. And now kids, be sure to come back to see what happens when Joseph meets his brothers, the same brothers who sold him into slavery.

END PART III

JOSEPH AND HIS BROTHERS: PART IV

(CHORUS *enters, sings Joseph song.*)

NARRATOR: Yes, this is the story of Joseph. If you remember, Joseph had been sold into slavery by his brothers and separated from his father, Jacob, who thought Joseph was dead. In Egypt, after being thrown in jail, Joseph had been released to interpret the dream of Pharaoh, the king of Egypt. The dream was that Egypt would experience seven years of plenty and after that seven years of starvation. The Lord interpreted the dream of Pharaoh through Joseph, and Pharaoh was so impressed that Joseph was put in charge of gathering the food and storing it away so that everybody would have something to eat during the seven years of famine.

(*Three* EGYPTIANS *enter chanting.*)

EGYPTIANS: Seven fat years, plenty to eat,
              Store up the grain and store up the wheat.
              Seven fat years, plenty of bread,
              Store up the grain, or we'll all be dead.

(*They exit.* EGYPTIAN 1 *enters with five loaves of bread.*)

EGYPTIAN 1: Ummm, bread, I love bread. Spread it thick with butter and jam. Or make a sandwich from tuna or ham. Yummy-yum.

(JOSEPH *enters. Takes one of the loaves.*)

JOSEPH: Thank you. This is for the seven years of hunger.

EGYPTIAN 1: My bread! All I can say, Joseph, is that if you're wrong, if we don't have seven years of hunger, you're going to be thrown back into jail where you belong.

(EGYPTIAN 1 *exits.* EGYPTIAN 2 *enters dragging loaded sack.*)

EGYPTIAN 2: Hee-hee. I've got all the extra wheat. I'll hide it from Joseph and keep it for myself. Hee-hee.

(JOSEPH *takes wheat from* EGYPTIAN 2.)

JOSEPH: Sorry, friend, all the extra food gets stored for the seven lean years to come.

EGYPTIAN 2: My wheat! All I can say, Joseph, is that if you're wrong and we don't have seven lean years, then you'll be the one that's sorry.

(EGYPTIAN 2 *exits.* EGYPTIAN 3 *enters with cutouts of bread, grapes, cakes, and turkeys.*)

EGYPTIAN 3: Party time. Come and get it. All the food you can eat. (*Handing food to kids*) Here, a turkey for you. And here's a cake for you.

(JOSEPH *enters and collects food.*)

JOSEPH: Party's over, I'm afraid. This has to be stored for the seven years of famine.

EGYPTIAN 3: Party pooper. All I can say, Joseph, is that if you're wrong, and we don't have seven years of famine, it will be your head.

(EGYPTIANS *cross over chanting "Seven Fat Years" dirge.*)

EGYPTIANS: The seven years of plenty are over, Joseph. You'd better be right about the seven lean years or else.

(*Start to advance on the unsuspecting* JOSEPH, *slowly, knives raised.* JOSEPH *is totaling up figures.*)

JOSEPH: Nine million tons of wheat, 30,000 sides of beef, figs, nuts, and one partridge in a pear tree.

(EGYPTIAN 2 *runs in just when stabbing is to take place.*)

EGYPTIAN 2: The famine has come. No rain. The crops and animals are dying. What'll we do?

(*Everyone runs around frantically.*)

JOSEPH: We'll praise the Lord and live off the food that we have stored away. All the world will starve. Egypt alone will have enough. I wonder how my father is getting on?

(JOSEPH *exits.* JACOB *enters.*)

JACOB: I'm Jacob, and I'm hungry. I'll call my sons—hey, boys, come out here!

(*The* BROTHERS *enter and go through the name routine, "I'm Reuben," etc.*)

Where's Joseph?

BROTHER 1: You remember, Father. Joseph was eaten by wild animals many years ago.

JACOB: Ah, yes, Joseph, dear Joseph. I want you all, except for little Benjamin, to go to Egypt and buy some grain and bring it back. I hear that they have stored up tons of the stuff. If we don't get any grain soon, we will starve to death. Well, don't just stand there, get moving.

(BROTHERS *perform a traveling routine in place as if they are walking a long distance.*)

BROTHERS: The famine is here, the famine is here.
                        There isn't any rain.
               The famine is here, the famine is here.
                        To Egypt to buy some grain.
               Over the sea, across the sand,
               We travel to get to Egypt land.

(JOSEPH *enters.*)

JOSEPH: What's this I see? My brothers. My brothers who threw me down a well and sold me into slavery.

BROTHER 2: Oh sir, will you sell us some grain?

(*They bow down before him.*)

JOSEPH (*to audience*): They don't recognize me. And look, they are bowing to me just as the Lord said they would in the dream. (*To* BROTHERS) How dare you come here to spy on the land of Egypt.

BROTHER 1: No, my lord, we are honest men. We come only to buy grain.

JOSEPH: Spies. You have come to spy on Egypt, to discover where we are weak. Throw them in the dungeon.

(*Tableau freeze.*)

NARRATOR: We have seen how the Lord blesses and preserves those who are faithful to Him. God also wants to bless and save each one of you if you will put your faith in His Son, Jesus Christ. Next time, we will find out how Joseph, a man of God, will treat his brothers, the same brothers who sold him into slavery. Will Joseph get revenge? Come back for the final episode in our exciting story of Joseph and His Brothers.

END PART IV

JOSEPH AND HIS BROTHERS: PART V

(BROTHERS *enter and sing the Joseph song.*)

NARRATOR: If you remember, Joseph had been sold into slavery by his brothers, who were jealous of the favor he had with their father, and he was taken to Egypt. But the Lord had watched over Joseph, and now he was the second most powerful man in the whole country. All the world was starving except for Egypt, for they had listened to Joseph when he told them to store grain for the hungry times ahead. Now Joseph's brothers had come to Egypt to buy grain to keep from starving. But they did not recognize their brother. What would Joseph do to them now? What would you do? Would you make them slaves? Would you want to get back at them? Let's see what happens.

(*Actors form tableau from previous sketch.*)

JOSEPH: Spies, you have come to spy on Egypt, to find out where we are weak. Throw them in the dungeon.

BROTHER 1: We are not spies. We're brothers, and all we want is food.

(*They go through the name routine.*)

BROTHER 2: We are 12 brothers, sons of Jacob from the land of Canaan.

JOSEPH: Twelve? I see only 10.

BROTHER 3: You see, Benjamin, the youngest, is still with our father, and Joseph, well, . . . you see . . . I mean . . . that is . . . er . . . Joseph is no more.

JOSEPH (*to audience):* They think I'm dead. (*To* BROTHERS) I'll tell you what. I'll keep Simeon here as a prisoner. (SIMEON *is bound.*) I'll get your grain, and you return to Canaan. Bring back this Benjamin brother of yours, and then I'll know you are telling the truth. But if you don't return, Simeon here will be put to death.

(*He exits.*)

BROTHER 1: Oh no, oh boy, oh woe is me, we're in for it now. Our father Jacob isn't going to like this at all. Benjamin is his favorite son.

BROTHER 3: None of this would have happened if we hadn't sold Joseph into slavery. The Lord is paying us back for our sins.

BROTHER 1: Let's go home and tell Jacob, our father.

(*They walk in place.*)

BROTHERS: Over the sea and across the land
                             We travel to get to our father's land.

(JACOB *enters.*)

JACOB: Oh, no.

BROTHERS: Oh, yes.

JACOB: It can't be.

BROTHERS: It is.

JACOB: I don't believe it.

BROTHERS: It's true.

JACOB: First Joseph, then Simeon, and now my youngest son, Benjamin. I won't do it. I won't let him go.

BROTHER 1: What do we do now?

JACOB: Let's eat, I'm hungry.
            (*They all gobble down food.* BROTHERS *exit.*)
        It's been many days now, and all our food is gone. Hey, sons, come out here. (BROTHERS *enter.*) Take little Benjamin here with you if you must. I guess I have to let you take him, or we will all starve to death. Go back to Egypt and buy more grain. May God be with you.

(*He exits.* BROTHERS *also exit chanting.*)

BROTHERS: Over the sea
                               Across the sand
                             We travel to get
                               To Egypt land.

(JOSEPH *enters and* BROTHERS *bow down.*)

JOSEPH: So you have returned. Is your old father, whom you spoke of, still alive? (BROTHERS *nod assent.*) So this is little Benjamin. May God be gracious to you, son. Now go inside. I have prepared a meal for you. (*They exit, leaving their sacks.*) Now I will test my brothers to see if God has changed their hearts. I will take this silver cup and hide it in Benjamin's sack, and we will see what happens.

(*The* BROTHERS *enter, rubbing their stomachs.*)

BROTHER 1: Ummmm good. Pyramid pie, my favorite.

BROTHER 2: Crocodile crumb cake—delicious.

JOSEPH: Now, take your grain and be off.

(*He exits.*)

BROTHERS: Over the sea across the land
                               We travel to get to . . .

(JOSEPH *enters.*)

JOSEPH: Stop! One of you has stolen my silver cup. Why have you repaid evil for good?

BROTHER 1: I assure you, Sire, none of us would do such a thing. But if we have, then you may kill the one who stole the cup, and the rest of us will be your slaves.

JOSEPH: So be it.
    (Searches through sacks. Each BROTHER *is relieved to find themselves innocent. Last of all he comes to* BENJAMIN *played by* BROTHER 2.)
    Ah-ha. The silver cup. *(The* BROTHERS *cower back in fear.)* It is not for me to take this one's life. I will keep him as my slave, and the rest of you can go free.

BROTHER 1: Sire, please listen to me. If we were to return to our old father, Jacob, without his youngest son, Benjamin, he would certainly die from grief. Let me take Benjamin's place. I will be your slave. Please let Benjamin return to his father.

(They all plead.)

JOSEPH: I see that God has changed your hearts. Don't you know who I am? I am your lost brother, Joseph.

BROTHERS *(amazed):* Joseph!

JOSEPH: My brothers, don't be afraid. It was not you who sent me to Egypt. It was God. He sent me here and raised me to a powerful position so that when the famine came, you could come to me for food, and all our family would survive and be blessed. Now go, return to our father. Bring him and all your families to live here, with me, in Egypt.

(They embrace.)

BROTHERS *(chanting quickly):*
                               Over the sea,
                                 Across the sand,
                               We travel to get
                                 To Father's land.
    Come on, Jacob.

JACOB: I'm coming. I'm coming. Praise the Lord.

JACOB AND BROTHERS: Over the sea,
                                 Across the sand,
                               We travel to get
                                 To Egypt land.

JACOB: Joseph, my son. May the Lord be praised.

JOSEPH: Jacob, my father.

(They embrace.)

JACOB: Let us all sing the Joseph song one last time.

(They do this dancing also. The following speech can be adapted to the special needs of your audience.)

NARRATOR: Did Joseph hate his brothers for what they had done to him? No, he loved them and forgave them. Yes, he loved them and forgave them because he knew that God loved and forgave him and had a special plan for his life. God had a plan for Joseph's life, and He has a plan for yours too. And do you want to know how you can find out about God's plan? I'll tell you. Find out about Jesus Christ, accept Him as your Savior, let Him come into your heart and rule your life. Jesus is the plan for your life, and only through knowing Jesus can you find out what an exciting life it is to be a Christian.

THE END

ABIDE IN THE LORD

Bible Verse: If a man does not abide in me, he is cast forth as a branch and withers; and the branches are gathered, thrown into the fire and burned. If you abide in me, and my words abide in you, ask whatever you will and it shall be done for you *(John 15:6-7, RSV).*

(MOSES *enters.)*

MOSES: Moses is my name. And these are my people, the Lord's people. Can you guess what they are working so hard at doing? They are building pyramids for the wicked Pharaoh of Egypt. They are slaves.

(PHARAOH *enters with* SLAVES. *He whips them.)*

PHARAOH: Pyramids, pyramids, build me more pyramids. I want a pyramid for me, a pyramid for my wives, and a pyramid for my cat, Tut-Tut. Build, you worthless slaves, build.

(He whips them. They scream. He exits.)

SLAVE 1: Nothing could be worse than this.

SLAVE 2: If only we were free.

JOASH *(to his wife):* Are you all right, Rebah?

REBAH: Oh Joash, I'm so tired. I don't think I can go on.

JOASH: Don't think, Rebah. Just work.

(SLAVES *exit moaning and groaning.)*

MOSES: But the Lord had sent me into Egypt to tell the wicked Pharaoh to set my people free. The Lord had not forgotten His people. The Lord showed His power by turning all the water to blood so that nobody could drink, but still the Pharaoh would not let my people go. The Lord will send a curse of frogs next. I want all of you to help by making frog sounds when I lift my staff like this. Let's practice. *(Encourages kids in response. To* PHARAOH, *who has entered)* Will you let my people go?

PHARAOH: No. I love my pyramids too much.

MOSES: Then the Lord will send frogs all across the land.

(MOSES *raises his staff. Kids respond.)*

PHARAOH: Eeeeeek! I hate frogs. I can't stand the sound of their croaking. All right, I'll let your people go.

(PHARAOH exits.)

MOSES: But then Pharaoh went back on his word. The next curse that the Lord would send would be flies. Can you make the sound of angry flies when I raise my staff? Good.

(PHARAOH enters.)

PHARAOH: Thank goodness those frogs are gone.

MOSES: Will you let my people go?

PHARAOH: No, no. I love my pyramids too much.

MOSES: Then the Lord will send swarms of flies all across the land.

(He raises his staff. Response from kids.)

PHARAOH: Oh, stop, ouch! *(Swats at flies)* All right, all right, I'll let your cursed people go.

(He exits.)

MOSES: But again the Pharaoh went back on his word. And after that, the Lord sent a plague that killed all the animals. *(Sound of dying animals comes from behind the curtain)* And the people were covered with boils. *(More sounds)* And the Lord rained down hailstones from the skies and locusts to destroy the land. And finally the Lord brought darkness over all of Egypt.

(PHARAOH enters.)

PHARAOH: I can't see. The sun disappeared. I can't see my beautiful pyramids.

MOSES: Will you let my people go now?

PHARAOH: Never, I tell you. Never!

MOSES: Then the Lord will cause the firstborn child of every man and every animal to die at midnight when the angel of death passes over.

PHARAOH: Bah!

(He exits. JOASH and REBAH enter.)

JOASH: Quick, Rebah, hurry into our house.

REBAH: What's wrong, Joash? What are you doing?

JOASH: I'm painting an X on our door so the angel of death will pass over our house and not destroy us.

REBAH: Oh, Joash, I'm frightened.

(They huddle together as screams are heard from offstage.)

JOASH: Don't be frightened. The Lord is with us.

(They exit. PHARAOH *enters carrying son.)*

PHARAOH: My son, my son is dead. Moses, you win. You and your God win. I'll let your people go.

(CROWD *enters.)*

CROWD: We're free. The Lord has set us free. We'll never complain again. On to the Promised Land.

REBAH: Joash, isn't it wonderful?

JOASH: We're free, Rebah. We're free.

MOSES: And the Lord sent a pillar of smoke and dust to lead us at daytime *(This can be done with scarves or crepe paper)* and a pillar of fire to guide us at night. And we walked. *(People walk with a good bit of energy.)* And we walked. *(People walk a bit more bent over.)* And we walked. *(People walk very slowly and start to grumble, variously.)*

CROWD: My back is killing me. Where is this so-called Promised Land? Promised Land, my eye—this desert goes on forever.

MOSES: But the Lord was angry with His people for grumbling, so He kept them in the desert. But every morning He gave them food that fell from heaven—manna.

JOASH: I'm beat, Rebah. What's for dinner?

REBAH: Well, we start with manna salad. Then we have some creamed manna, and for dessert—a big helping of fried manna.

JOASH: I'm going to turn into a manniac if I have to eat anymore manna. Remember how great it was in Egypt?

REBAH: But we were slaves in Egypt!

JOASH: Yes, but we had watermelons to eat.

REBAH: Yes.

JOASH: And sweet succulent corn.

REBAH: Yes.

JOASH: And tasty chicken meat.

REBAH: Oh, yes.

JOASH: Let's leave the tribes, Rebah. We could do much better on our own. Who needs the Lord and His silly manna?

REBAH: Yes, let's go.

(They pack and move to the opposite side of the playing area.)

MOSES: And the two young ones left us. Watch what happens to them.

JOASH: We're free, Rebah. No more manna.

REBAH: No more pillar of fire. No more walking in circles in the desert. We can make it on our own.

(They dance around together.)

MOSES: And so a couple of days went by.

JOASH: What's for dinner?

REBAH: Nothing.

JOASH: Not even any manna?

REBAH: The manna goes with the Lord.

JOASH: Well, anyway, it sure is good to be on our own isn't it? *(Silence from RE-BAH)* Look at those silly people still following that pillar of fire.

REBAH: It's so dark out.

JOASH: That's because the fire left us.

REBAH: And cold.

JOASH: I told you, that's because the fire has left us.

REBAH: You don't have to get angry and shout.

(Silence)

JOASH: I'm sorry.

REBAH: And I'm thirsty.

JOASH: The Lord would always help Moses get water for us.

REBAH: What are we doing? Let's go back to the Lord.

JOASH: Yes, let's.

(They exit with CROWD.)

MOSES: So Rebah and Joash came back to the Lord. You know, kids, a lot of people try to make it on their own without the Lord, without Jesus. But remember—it's a cold world without the Lord Jesus, and it's dark and lonely. Jesus is the light of this world, and when you have asked Jesus into your heart, you will never be alone.

THE END

LOVE GOD MORE THAN YOURSELF

Bible Verse: You shall love the Lord your God with all your heart, and with all your soul, . . . and with all your mind *(Luke 10:27, RSV).*

(COMPANY enters and sings "Samson Song.")

SAMSON SONG
Oh, Samson, Samson, Samson,
  You were the strongest one of all.
Oh, Samson, Samson, Samson,
  Why, tell me, did you fall?
Oh, Samson, Samson, Samson,
  Delilah led you astray.
Oh, Samson, Samson, Samson,
  It's the Lord you should obey.
Oh, Samson, Samson, Samson,
  Don't let 'em cut your hair,
Oh, Samson, Samson, Samson,
  Don't you act on a dare.
Oh, Samson, Samson, Samson,
  You should love yourself a bit less.
Oh, Samson, Samson, Samson,
  Now you've got yourself in a mess.
Oh, Samson, Samson, Samson,
  Love the Lord with all your might.
Oh, Samson, Samson, Samson,
  Love your Lord 'cause He is right.

NARRATOR: A long time ago, there lived a man named Samson. Samson was a Nazirite, which meant that he was a special servant of the Lord. And when he was born, the Lord told his mother that Samson should never cut his hair. Well, Samson grew to be a handsome, fine, strong man, and like a lot of handsome, fine, strong men, he was pretty full of himself.

(SAMSON enters with ADMIRERS, who "ohhh" and "ahhh" when he flexes his muscles.)

SAMSON: Hey, did I ever tell you the one about how I finished off 1,000 Philistines with nothing but the jawbone of a donkey?

ADMIRER 1: You did, Samson?

SAMSON: Well, I guess the Lord gave me a helping hand. (ADMIRERS *laugh.*)

Anyway, I bent down and picked up the jawbone of a donkey. There I was, faced with all those spears and angry faces. But do you think I was afraid? *Wap! Sonk! Kapowee!* One thousand Philistines lay dead at my feet. Er—I mean, it was the Lord who did it all. It was the Lord who gave me my might.

ADMIRER 1: That must have been a terrible sight. But tell me, Samson, it wasn't all the Lord. You must have done a little bit yourself.

SAMSON: Well, if you want to know, I'm not exactly a weakling you know. After all, 1,000 dead, let me tell you.

(They all exit. PHILISTINES *enter chanting, "We hate Samson.")*

PHILISTINES: We're Philistines, and we hate Samson.

PHILISTINE 1: Wait until I get my hands on him.

PHILISTINE 2: I'd like to tear him limb from limb.

PHILISTINE 3: Wait until I get my hands on him.

SAMSON *(appearing suddenly):* Hi, Philistines.

*(*PHILISTINES *cower in a heap.)*

PHILISTINES: Help, it's him. Don't hurt us, Samson.

*(*SAMSON *exits laughing.* DELILAH *enters to whistles from* PHILISTINES.*)*

DELILAH: Now is that anyway for a Philistine to act?

PHILISTINE 1: Delilah, help us find out what makes Samson so strong.

PHILISTINE 2: Delilah, we want to get him back for doing us wrong.

PHILISTINE 3: Delilah, we'll pay you to help us find out what makes Samson so strong.

DELILAH: Did I hear somebody mention money?

PHILISTINES: Lots of money!

DELILAH: All I have to do is find out what makes him so strong? That shouldn't take long.

PHILISTINES: Oh, thank you. You're number one, Delilah. Thank you.

*(*PHILISTINES *exit.* SAMSON *enters flexing.)*

DELILAH: Hi ya, handsome. Excuse me for seeming fresh, but do you think you will allow little ol' me to feel that great big muscle on your arm?

SAMSON: Sure. *(Flexes)* Say, you're kinda cute.

DELILAH: You're not so bad looking yourself, big boy. And you're so strong I don't think anyone could capture you. Tell me, why are you so strong?

SAMSON: Well, if I were tied with seven raw-leather bowstrings, I would become as weak as anyone else.

DELILAH: Really? Go to sleep you man mountain, you.
> (PHILISTINES *creep in with strings.* DELILAH *ties up* SAMSON. PHILISTINES *are ready to pounce with knives.*)
> Samson! The Philistines are here!
> (*He snaps the bowstrings and beats* PHILISTINES *off.*)
> You are making fun of me! You told me a lie. Please tell me how you can be captured.

SAMSON: Well, if you tied me with brand-new ropes that have never been used, I will be as weak as other men.

DELILAH: Really? Go to sleep you man mountain, you.
> (PHILISTINES *creep in with ropes.* DELILAH *ties him up.*)
> Samson, the Philistines have come to capture you!
> (SAMSON *breaks ropes.* PHILISTINES *flee.*)
> You have mocked me again and told me more lies! Now tell me how you can really be captured. How can you say you love me when you don't confide in me?

SAMSON: All right! All right! (*Looks around as he tells secret*) My hair has never been cut, for I've been a Nazirite to God since before my birth. If my hair were cut, my strength would leave me, and I would become as weak as anyone else.

DELILAH: Really? Go to sleep you man mountain, you.

(PHILISTINES *creep in with scissors.* SAMSON'S *hair is cut. A wig is taken off.* DELILAH *hits* SAMSON *and wakes him up. He can't defend himself.* DELILAH *and* PHILISTINES *laugh. Money is exchanged. They blind* SAMSON *and put chains on him.*)

PHILISTINE 1: Our god Dagon has delivered our enemy to us.

PHILISTINE 2: Let's go to the temple and have a big party and celebrate.

PHILISTINE 3: Yeah, let's celebrate.

(REVELERS *come on with reveling props. They laugh at* SAMSON *and make fun of him.*)

REVELERS (*ad-lib*): Where's all you strength now, big boy? (*And so on.*)

SAMSON: Place my hands against the two pillars. I want to rest them.
> (REVELERS *do this on cardboard cutouts of columns.* SAMSON *prays.*)
> O Lord, I ask Your forgiveness. I forgot You and thought only of myself. You are my strength, O Lord. O Lord Jehovah, remember me again—please strengthen me one more time so that I may pay back the Philistines for the loss of at least one of my eyes. (*Trembles*) My strength is returning.

(SAMSON *pushes, and the pillars come crashing down.*)

NARRATOR: And all the wicked Philistines died that day. Samson died too, but he died asking the Lord for forgiveness. Remember, kids, that Jesus wants you to love the Lord with all your heart, soul, and mind. Samson let Delilah lead him away from the Lord. If you really love Jesus, nothing can lead you away from the Father.

THE END

JONAH AND THE LORD

NARRATOR: This is a story about Jonah and a big fish. Jonah was a prophet of God. You know, many of the prophets that God spoke to really jumped when the Lord commanded them to do something. Elijah took on 450 prophets of Baal. Daniel wasn't afraid to be thrown to the lions for praying to his Lord; and Jeremiah, when he told the people to repent, made them so mad that they threw him into a slimy pit. But what about Jonah? Did Jonah do what the Lord asked him to do? No. Jonah ran away from the Lord.

SINGERS:
> Jonah was a dropout—boom, boom.
> Jonah, he copped out—boom, boom.
> Jonah took a boat—boom, boom—
> That wouldn't stay afloat—boom, boom.
> The Lord sent a fish
> Because it was His wish
> To send Jonah to the bottom of the sea,
> Swish, swish, swish. *(Repeat)*

(JONAH sneaks in.)

JONAH: Shhh! I'm running from the Lord. Will you hide me? *(JONAH tries to hide among the kids.)* It's no use. How can I hide from the Lord. *(To kids)* Will He see me over here, or under here, or what if I make a funny face? There must be some place I can hide from Him. Do you know why I am running away from the Lord? The Lord told me that I should tell the people from Nineveh that the Lord was going to destroy them for their wickedness and that they should repent. Well, can you imagine me, a foreigner, walking into that evil city over there and telling those people that the Lord is going to destroy them? They would probably laugh at me. They could very easily throw me out of the city. They might even kill me. Look, here come some of them now.

(NINEVITES enter, carousing and wicked.)

NINEVITES:
> We're from Nineveh,
> And our favorite word is
> Bah! Bah! Bah!

KING: And who might this be?

JONAH: My name is Jonah.

NINEVITES: Jonah? *(Laugh.)*

KING: And what might you have to say—Jonah?

(NINEVITES *laugh.* KING *cuts them off with a gesture.*)

JONAH: The Lord sent me to tell you . . .

NINEVITES: Yes?

JONAH: Nothing. (NINEVITES *exit laughing.*) Do you see what I mean? I know the Lord is watching me, but I just can't go through with it.

(The following sequence in brackets is sung in ascending minors.)

[LORD: Jonah!

JONAH: Are You talking to me?

LORD: Jonah!

JONAH: Can't You see I'm busy?

LORD: Jonah!

JONAH: Oh, Lord, leave me alone.

LORD: Jonah!]

JONAH: I just want to go home. I know, I'll run away to sea. The Lord will never be able to catch me.

(CREW *enters with cutout of ship, sail, etc.*)

CREW *(singing):* Sailing, sailing, over the ocean blue . . .

CAPTAIN: I am the captain, and this is my crew.

JONAH: So I got on board ship and sailed far away. Everything went all right for a while, and I thought I had given the slip to the Lord. But can you run away from the Lord? *(Response)* Anyway, I went to sleep, but the Lord sent a big storm.

CAPTAIN: Storm, ahoy.

CREW: Storm, ahoy.

CAPTAIN: Big storm, ahoy.

CREW: Big storm, ahoy.

CAPTAIN: Monstrous storm, ahoy!

CREW: Help! Help! Help!

CAPTAIN: Everybody pray to your gods. *(They pray. A lot of mumbo jumbo.)* It's no use. Throw the cargo overboard. Wait a minute. *(Points to* JONAH*)* Wake him up. Why didn't you pray to your God when the storm came up?

JONAH: I can't pray to my God. I'm running away from Him.

CAPTAIN: Who are you?

JONAH: I'm a Jew.

CAPTAIN: Humph! I don't like the looks of this. I know, we'll draw straws to see who has offended their gods. The one who gets the short straw, loses. *(They draw straws. JONAH loses.)* So you are the guilty one! What are we going to do with you?

JONAH: Throw me overboard. It's the only way to save the ship.

CAPTAIN: How dare you make such a suggestion! I have never lost a ship. I've never lost a crewman, and I've never lost a passenger. But I guess there is a first time for everything. Throw him overboard.

(CREW throws JONAH overboard after swinging him to the count of three.)

JONAH: And I sank down into the water—down, down I went until I thought my lungs would burst. Down through the light blue water, down through the dark blue water, down through the black, black water. And just when I thought I would die, a huge fish swam along and swallowed me whole.
(Fish made from crepe paper and cardboard and supported by actors "swallows" JONAH.)
Have you ever been in the belly of a big fish? Well, let me tell you it's pretty icky and slimy and pitch dark. But after three days, I realized that the Lord had spared me. *(On his knees)* Lord, I will surely fulfill Your request. I'll go any place You ask, Lord. I'll go to the stinkiest swamp. I'll go to the Arctic. I'll even go to . . . I'll even go to . . . Nineveh. And the fish spat me out onto dry land. *(JONAH comes out of the fish. Fish exits.)* And do you know what I did? I ran straight to Nineveh. Uh oh, here they come now.

NINEVITES: We're from Nineveh
                        And our favorite word is
                        Bah! Bah! Bah!

JONAH: We'll, here goes. You people are wicked. You are sinful. You are an ugly sight to the Lord. The Lord told me to tell you that in 40 days, your city will be destroyed. I tell you, your city will be destroyed. *(Turning away)* I can't bear to look. *(To kids)* Are they laughing at me? *(Response)* Are the sneaking up on me to beat me? *(Response)* Are they still doing wicked things?

(Response. By this time, all the people of Nineveh are down on their knees.)

KING: We repent of our sins, Lord. We thank You for Your message and for Your messenger, Jonah. We all say . . .

NINEVITES: Praise the Lord!

(They celebrate. JONAH just shakes his head.)

NARRATOR: And do you know that the Lord spared Nineveh? Yes, He spared the city because they said they were sorry. Now, Jonah was in the belly of that fish for three days and three nights, and the Lord spared Jonah; and after Jonah told the people to repent, He spared the city of Nineveh. He spared Jonah. He spared Nineveh. But did He spare His own Son, Jesus? No. He let Jesus die on the Cross and then brought Him back to life on the third day. Jesus died—not just so that every man or even a city might be spared—He died so that everybody . . . you, me, everybody might be saved if they believe in Him. And that, boys and girls, is good news!

THE END

DAVID: PART I— ANOINTING OF DAVID

Bible Verse: Man looks on the outward appearance; but the LORD looks on the heart *(1 Samuel 16:7, RSV).*

(SAMUEL, a crusty-looking prophet figure, enters. He reads a street sign.)

SAMUEL: Bethlehem! Well, it could be worse. *(Rubs his feet)* The Lord has me traveling all over the country, and at my age—but when He calls, these old bones got to get going. He's brought me here to anoint the future king of Israel—one of the sons of Jesse, I'm told. Well, no use wasting my wind here. Better be getting on to see Jesse, I guessy.

(He exits. JESSE enters.)

JESSE: Hey, sons, git out here.
> *(His sons enter. DAVID comes in last and stands separate from the others.)*
> Now, it's time we got this here household moving along. I hear the prophet Samuel's going to visit our house sometime today, and I want everything looking spic and span. Eliab, I want you to clean the house.

ELIAB: Really, Father, must I? I have spent years cultivating my brain to dwell on the higher things, like the movement of the stars and advanced mathematics. I'd much prefer spending the day in the library where I can bask in the brilliance of my brain.

JESSE: Ye'll do it. *(Hands him broom)*

ELIAB: All right, all right, if you insist. Just as long as I don't have to take care of those vermin-ridden sheep. *(Brothers "ugh," all except DAVID)* How do you get one of these things to work?

JESSE: Shammah, I want you to clean the barn. *(Hands him a shovel)*

SHAMMAH: Oh, Father, please. I'm much too delicate. You know how I get palpitations and cold sweats when I have to exert myself—I'm also frightened of dark musty corners.

JESSE: Git.

SHAMMAH: All right, just as long as I don't have to tend those smelly sheep.

(Brothers "ugh" again.)

JESSE: Abinadab, you skedaddle down town and bring back some goat's milk and sour bread.

ABINADAB: Sorry, Father, but my schedule does not permit me doing that at this time. Can't tamper with my schedule. Let's see, I'm jogging this morning until 10. Then I'm lifting weights until 12, after which I'm spending 45 minutes flexing my back muscles for the local ladies—I'm all booked up.

JESSE: Yer goin' all right.

ABINADAB: You know what happens to me if I can't follow my schedule—I go to pieces. (JESSE *threatens him with a wooden bucket.*) OK, I'm off, just as long as I don't have to shepherd those mangy sheep.

(Brothers "ugh" a third time.)

JESSE: David, you're the youngest. You tend the sheep.

DAVID: Yes, Father.

JESSE: No complaints?

DAVID: None. In fact, I like those simple creatures. I also like the hills where they graze—never a dull moment what with wolves and lions—but I've been practicing with this. *(Gets out slingshot)* I also need to find time to write songs to the Lord.

ABINADAB: He's flipped his wig.

ELIAB: He's obviously deranged.

SHAMMAH: He's no brother of mine.

JESSE: Git.

(All exit but JESSE. SAMUEL *enters.)*

SAMUEL: Howdy, Jesse.

JESSE: Mornin', Sam. Hot enough for ye?

SAMUEL: Yep. Supposed to rain a spell this afternoon. Got the hay in?

JESSE: Yep. What brings you to these parts?

SAMUEL: Why the Lord, of course. Wants me to give a special blessing to one of yer sons.

JESSE: Ain't that somethin'. Which one is it?

SAMUEL: Well, I don't rightly know. Why don't you bring them all out, and we'll let the Lord tell me.

JESSE: Good idea. Hey, sons, come out here. The prophet Samuel is here, and he's goin' to give one of you a very special blessing. Come on, git, soweeeeeee!

(ELIAB runs out with broom in one hand and book in the other.)

ELIAB: Here I am, Father. I'm ready for the blessing.

JESSE: This here is Eliab. He's got all the brains in the family.

ELIAB: The area of a triangle is determined by . . . (*He starts a string of formulas and multiplication tables. This could be a place for audience participation, depending on the composition of your audience. He could get stuck on one of the multiplication tables: "Six times seven is . . . is . . . can you help?" Audience yells out, "Forty-two," and he says, "Thanks, just testing you out."*)

SAMUEL: Why, he's one smart cookie. (*Looks up*) This must be the one, Lord. He's a smart one, all right.

GOD'S VOICE (*over a speaker*): Samuel, pay no attention to this man's worldly wisdom. He's not the one. Man looks at the outward appearance, but I look at the heart.

SAMUEL: Sorry, Jesse, he's not the one.

(SHAMMAH *runs out sneezing.*)

SHAMMAH: I'm here for the special anointing, Father. Eeeyou. All that dust has set me fluttering. Look what it's done to my curls.

JESSE: This here's Shammah. He's a handsome fellow.

SAMUEL: He'd make a right handsome king. Well, Lord, this looks like our man.

GOD'S VOICE: Samuel, I do not judge as man judges. He is not the one.

SAMUEL: Oh. Sorry, Jess—who else you got around?

(ABINADAB *enters with a girl on each arm admiring his muscles.*)

ABINADAB: Easy now, look but don't touch. Here I am, Father. Let's see, I'll be ready for the blessing at 3:05 this afternoon if it doesn't last any longer than six minutes.

JESSE: This is Abinadab. He's so strong he can carry nine sacks of grain without even flinching.

SAMUEL: Hey, Lord, You've really picked yerself a winner here. He's as strong as an ox.

GOD'S VOICE: Samuel, how many times must I tell you. Man looks on the outward appearance. I look on the heart.

SAMUEL: The Lord passed him by too, Jess. Anybody else around?

JESSE: Nobody that would be right, I'm afraid.

(*This following section can be done in two ways: one participational and one straight. The participational way would have* SAMUEL *coming out and talking to the audience.*)

[SAMUEL: Well, the Lord seems to have led me astray. He's rejected those fine boys there. Do you know of anyone who might be deserving of the Lord's blessing? Who? David? Hey, Jesse, you never told me you had a son named David.]

(Or the straight way)

[SAMUEL: Now Jesse, think real hard. You got any more sons?

JESSE: Well, he's awful young, and he's tending the sheep right now, and he doesn't look much like a king—but I do have one more son, and his name is David.]

(Resume play.)

ELIAB, SHAMMAH, AND ABINADAB: David? You must be kidding.

ELIAB: He doesn't even know his multiplication tables yet.

SHAMMAH: He's cute, but not handsome like me.

ABINADAB: I'm twice, no, three times as strong as him.

SAMUEL: Well, go git him, would ye?

(They all exit, JESSE yelling for DAVID and the three sons grumbling. DAVID enters with sheep. He is up in the hills. The sheep can be played by kids on all fours baaing.)

DAVID: The Lord is my Shepherd and He takes care of me. No, that's not quite right. Ahh, yes, "The Lord is my Shepherd; I shall not want. He makes me . . . He makes me . . ."

(Audience participation as DAVID asks them to help him finish line. JESSE's voice is heard as if in the distance.)

JESSE: David, David, come down from those hills.

DAVID: That's my father calling. I'll leave the song until later, not that it will ever amount to much. Come on, sheep.

(He exits, the sheep following. JESSE and family and SAMUEL enter from one side, DAVID from the other.)

JESSE: This is my youngest son, David.

ABINADAB: Phew! He smells of sheep.

SHAMMAH: Look at those clothes, would you?

ELIAB: Once a shepherd, always a shepherd.

SAMUEL: Well, Lord?

GOD'S VOICE: This is the one—anoint him.

(D*AVID* kneels. S*AMUEL* approaches with oil. Tableau freezes as S*AMUEL* speaks.)

S*AMUEL*: So you see, God requires certain qualities from those He asks to serve Him, and the most important of these are those that come from deep within. David was obedient—obedient to his father and to his Lord. David was humble—he didn't walk around all puffed up with how great he was. And last but not least, David loved the Lord, sang songs to Him, and loved to serve Him. So, all of you remember . . .

(Tableau unfreezes.)

A*LL*: Man looks at the outward appearance, but God looks at the heart. God is a Judge of people, and He is a good Judge, for He knows us like we truly are.

END PART I

DAVID: PART II— DAVID AND GOLIATH

Bible Verse: O Lord, you alone are my hope; I've trusted you from childhood (*Psalm 71:5*, TLB).

(SOLDIERS *enter. While they talk,* GOLIATH *appears in the background.* GOLIATH *can be made by using a blanket and putting one actor on the shoulders of another actor or by using a large puppet.*)

SOLDIER 1: I'm an Israeli soldier. Nothing frightens me.

SOLDIER 2: Yeah, we're soldiers in King Saul's army. Nothing frightens us.

SOLDIER 3: I could lick the entire Philistine army with one arm tied behind my back. Do you believe me, kids?

(MESSENGER *runs on.*)

MESSENGER: Stop admiring your muscles. Have you guys seen him yet?

SOLDIERS: Seen who?

MESSENGER: The Philistines have a giant on their side. He's challenging anyone in our army to fight with him. He's nine feet tall.

SOLDIER 1: If he's nine feet tall, then I'm a monkey's uncle.

MESSENGER: His spear is as thick as my leg.

SOLDIER 2: If his spear is that thick, then I'm a ring-tailed anteater.

MESSENGER: And he wears armor that weighs over 120 pounds.

SOLDIER 3: If his armor weighs that much, then I'm a chocolate chip cookie in a herd of cookie monsters.

(GOLIATH *enters.*)

GOLIATH: Hey, guys.

ALL: Oh, no!

(*They say this line frightened without looking at* GOLIATH.)

GOLIATH: Turn around. (*They slowly turn around.*) BOO!

ALL: I thought I saw a Goliath giant.

(They scream and exit.)

GOLIATH: Cowards! You quivering Israelites. Why do you run? Are you frightened of my massive height or my massive muscles or of my massive mentality? You choose one of your men to fight me. If he wins and kills me, we will be your slaves; but if I win and kill him, you will be our slaves. Here and now I challenge you, a fight to the death. You'd think I had bad breath or something.

(He laughs and exits. SAUL enters.)

SAUL: I, King Saul, mighty ruler of all the armies of Israel, offer a reward to anyone who can kill the giant Goliath.

(CROWD enters frightened. DAVID is with them.)

DAVID *(to audience):* I have been up in the mountains tending my sheep. My brothers and my father say that I am too young to be a soldier. I have never seen this Goliath, but he must be a terrible fighter to have frightened everyone. But if you have God on your side, what do you have to fear?

SAUL: I will give much money to the man who will fight Goliath. I will give him my daughter in marriage. I will even allow that person not to pay any income tax. Now anyone who wants to fight Goliath, please take one giant step forward.
    (Everyone takes one step back, except for DAVID.)
    Please, won't one of my soldiers take a step forward?
    (Everyone takes another step back. DAVID steps forward.)
    Aren't you afraid of Goliath?

DAVID: Your majesty, no one should be afraid of this Philistine. I will go and fight him.

SAUL: But how can you fight him? You are but a mere boy. He is a giant soldier.

DAVID: Your majesty, I take care of my father's sheep. I have attacked lions and bears going after my sheep. And if the lion or bear turns on me, I grab it by the throat and beat it to death. If the Lord has saved me from lions and bears, He will save me from Goliath.

SAUL: I have never let a boy near the front line of battle. I have never let a boy be a soldier in my army. I have never let a boy do my fighting for me. But I guess there's a first time for everything. Here, take my armor. Here's my trusty sword, my trusty helmet, my trusty shield.

(DAVID puts on armor. During his speech, he takes it all off.)

DAVID: Wait. The Lord does not need swords or spears to save His people. All I need is Him. With my trusty slingshot and with the Lord's help that giant will fall. All I need is five smooth stones.

(He bends to pick them up.)

SOLDIER 1: OK, David, you can stop pretending now. Why don't you run back to your sheep before you get turned into Cream of Wheat?

DAVID *(stands):* Five. Now, show me where this giant is.

SAUL AND SOLDIERS: It was nice knowing you, David.

SAUL: I can't look.

(GOLIATH enters.)

GOLIATH: Ho! Ho! Ho! I smell the blood of an Israelite. But where is he? I can't see him.

DAVID: Here I am. Down here.

GOLIATH: But you are only a child. I could chew you up in one bite. Look at this spear. Look at me.

DAVID: You come to me with spear and shield, but I come to fight you in the name of the Lord.

GOLIATH: Ha! I sneeze on your Lord. Achoo! Come here, you little snipe. I will make dog food out of you.

DAVID: Lord, You are my hope. I have trusted in You since childhood. Give me strength.

(They fight. GOLIATH dies. SAUL approaches audience.)

SAUL: Has Goliath killed young David yet? Was he torn limb from limb? I can't stand the sight of blood, would you tell me when Goliath has turned him into mincemeat? *(Response throughout)* What's that? He's still alive? David, you have killed the giant.

DAVID: It wasn't me, Saul. It was the Lord. Praise the Lord. The Lord has been with me since I was this high. He has helped me when I was afraid. *(To audience)* You know, most of you will never have to fight a giant in your lifetime, but you will have a lot of difficult times—times of fear and times of sadness. And our Father in heaven will always be there to help you like He helped me. Well, I have to get back to my sheep. Good-bye.

(He exits.)

END PART II

DAVID: PART III—
DAVID IN SAUL'S COURT

NARRATOR: Today, we will tell a story about the difference between two kings. One king thought that to be king he had to be number one and boss everyone around. . . . The other king—well, you just wait and see about the other king.

> Here are two objects. A spear . . .
> *(A spear is brought in.)*
> . . . and a lyre.
> *(A lyre is brought in. This can be made out of cardboard and string, or a guitar can be used and the word changed to "guitar.")*
> Now let me ask you—what is the difference between the spear and this lyre? What does a spear do? *(Response from audience)* That's right—it kills. It destroys. It's a weapon. And now—what does a lyre do? *(Response)* It makes music. Look at their different shapes—one sharp and pointed, one smooth and gently curved. Let me ask you, if you were an angry person, full of jealousy and hate, who always wants to boss others around, which of these objects might you want to use? The spear, of course . . .

(SAUL enters.)

SAUL *(taking spear):* Give me that.

NARRATOR: And if you were a man who loved the Lord, who was at peace with himself and liked to serve others, you might want to play this.

DAVID *(enters, takes lyre):* I will make a song unto the Lord. *(Sings or chants)* The Lord is my Shepherd; I shall not want.

NARRATOR: And so we meet two men, one king named Saul.

SAUL *(rages):* Arrrghhh.

NARRATOR: And one a young soldier named David.

DAVID: He makes me to lie down in green pastures.

(He exits.)

NARRATOR: One of them has turned from God, and one has remained true. One thinks he has to boss everybody around to be king; the other . . . well, let's see what happens.

CROWD *(off, chanting):* Saul has killed thousands, but David tens of thousands.

(SAUL enters.)

SAUL: Listen to them. They cheer David for killing more of those nasty Philistines than me. I never should have made him a general in my army. He's more popular than I am. He makes me so mad I could . . . *(Slams spear into foot. Yells, hops about.)* What are you laughing at? I suppose you're on David's side too, why you little . . .

(DAVID *enters with* CROWD *that is chanting. He carries lyre.)*

Look, even my son Jonathan embraces him.

JONATHAN *(enters):* David, it's so good to see you.

DAVID: And you too, Jonathan.

JONATHAN: Thank the Lord that you're safe.

DAVID: He has brought me through many a battle. I serve Him always, and He has told me to serve others too. *(Holding up lyre)* Now it's time to praise Him through song.

JONATHAN: Here, as a token of our friendship, take this robe. May nothing ever come between us. I am your servant.

DAVID: And I am yours.

(They do a fancy and involved handshake.)

JONATHAN AND DAVID: Yeah.

MICHEL *(entering):* David, you're safe.

DAVID: Of course. God is all powerful, and I am serving Him! What can I do for you today?

MICHEL: Oh, David, you are always so thoughtful!

SAUL: Look, even my daughter Michel runs to him. I think he's sweet on her also. That gives me an idea. *(Approaching* DAVID*)* Well, David, back from the wars, I see. Congratulations on your success. In appreciation for what you've done, I offer you the hand of my daughter, Michel, in marriage.

MICHEL *(hugging* SAUL*):* Oh, Daddy!

DAVID: But Sire, I am only your servant. I am not worthy.

SAUL: I will give you Michel's hand in marriage if you can kill 200 of those dreaded Philistines, enemies of my kingdom.

DAVID: Whoopee! Whatever you say, I'll do it! I am your servant. I better not be late; I've got a date with 200 unlucky Philistines. Come on, army. *(Exits)*

SAUL: He'll be slaughtered for sure—uh-oh, listen to that racket.

(Screams, cries. Helmets and swords flying about. DAVID *enters brushing off dust.)*

Is he dead yet? *(Audience response)* What's that? He's alive?

DAVID: It's done, king. Whatever you ask, I will do it. I'm your servant always. See you in church!

(CROWD *exits, everybody singing "Here Comes the Bride."*)

MICHEL: Oh, David, you did it. Let's go pick out our wedding rings.

DAVID: For you, Michel, I will do anything. I am always your servant.

(DAVID *and* MICHEL *exit.*)

SAUL *(alone onstage):* Why does everybody follow David? I ask you, what does he have that I don't have? I'm the king! Everyone does what I say, even him! He goes around helping other people like a slave. . . . He even sings music like a servant. . . . Oh, phooey, my head hurts. I'll call my servants. Hey, Plop. Hey, Fizz.

PLOP AND FIZZ *(entering):* Yes, Sire.

SAUL: Bring me relief. R-E-L-I-E-F. My head hurts.

PLOP: Poor King Saul, an evil spirit keeps him awake at night.

FIZZ: Probably jealousy.

PLOP: Sire, why don't you ask David to come play his lyre for you. Remember, music soothes the savage soul of even the mightiest beast.

SAUL: Good idea. *(Calling)* David—

DAVID: Yes, your majesty?

SAUL: Play your harp and sing for me.

DAVID: Sure thing, king, anything you say, for I am your servant.

(SAUL *gets madder and madder and finally picks up his spear to throw at* DAVID *as he sings one of the psalms. They all freeze.*)

NARRATOR: How are these two people different? Saul likes to be big a shot and always boss people around. But what is different about David? *(Gets answer from kids. He is a servant.)* That's right. David, though he had been anointed as a king by Samuel, decided to serve others and not be bossy. Come back next time to find out about what happens to David.

END PART III

DAVID: PART IV—DAVID AND JONATHAN, FRIENDS

NARRATOR: You remember our story so far, that David kept serving his friends, his Lord, and even his king . . . and this made Saul pretty mad . . . so mad that as David sang to him, he picked up a spear and was about to skewer him! Today's story is about best friends. Let's watch and see who David's best friend is.

SAUL *(entering):* I'll pin him to the wall.

(SAUL throws spear and misses. DAVID grabs the spear. For a second he hesitates, then throws the spear down and grabs lyre and exits.)

What have I done? David, David come back.

(He exits, dragging sword. DAVID runs on.)

DAVID *(to audience):* Saul is certainly mad. Will you hide me?

(He hides in audience. JONATHAN enters.)

JONATHAN: David? David, where are you?

DAVID: It's Jonathan, my friend. Should I go to him? Jonathan is King Saul's son. . . . Maybe he's mad too. After all, he ought to be the new king after Saul, but God has said that I will be the new king. What if Jonathan is looking to stab me too? What do you think? *(Audience response)* Well, he is my best friend. I think I'll give him a chance. *(To JONATHAN)* Over here, Jonathan.

JONATHAN: David, we are going to celebrate the feast of the New Moon. We have a place set for you next to Father. Come on, we're having barbecued chicken and chocolate cream pie.

DAVID: If I came, I'd be the barbecued chicken. Saul wants me dead.

JONATHAN: That's crazy. He tells me everything, and he's never said . . . it just isn't so.

DAVID: Go back and ask him.

JONATHAN: I will.

DAVID: Wait. How will you let me know if Saul is over his madness or if he wants to serve me up for dessert? He'll be watching you closely.

JONATHAN: I tell you what. I'll shoot an arrow, and when my servant goes to pick it up, I will tell him to go further on past you. That will be a warning that you are in danger. If I tell him that the arrow is on this side of you—then all is well.

DAVID: But your father will not like it if you tip me off.

JONATHAN: You are my friend. With you, I will be honest and true, and I will do my best to protect you. That's what friends are for.

DAVID: Good. *(Doing elaborate handshake)* You are a true friend.

(DAVID hides. JONATHAN exits. SAUL enters.)

SAUL: Arghhh. *(JONATHAN enters, and SAUL grabs him.)* You young whipper-snapper! You've been off seeing that friend of yours, David. Haven't you?

JONATHAN: Yes. But what has he done to you? He is a friend to both of us. He is your servant and always will be . . .

SAUL: You fool, don't you realize that as long as David is alive you will never be king of this country? God favors him.

JONATHAN: He's still my friend.

SAUL: He should be your enemy. You should be jealous and hate him. Now go and bring him to me.

JONATHAN: But jealousy and hatred never helped anyone. If God wants David to be king, then it will happen, whether you or I want it to or not.

SAUL: Go!

(Threatens with spear. JONATHAN runs out, taking bow and arrow. SERVANT follows. SAUL sneaks back to watch, spear in hand.)

JONATHAN: Run and find the arrow I'm going to shoot.

(He shoots. SERVANT runs to arrow.)

NARRATOR: Now will Jonathan warn David, or will he obey his father, the king? What do you think? *(Audience response)* Let's see what happens.

JONATHAN: The arrow is further on. Go further.

DAVID: That's the warning. I'm out of here!

(He exits.)

SAUL *(to audience)*: Have you seen David anyplace? *(Exiting)* Curses!

JONATHAN: God be with you, David. The Lord will make sure that you and I will forever keep the sacred promise of friendship we have made to each other.

NARRATOR: And do you know that God has made each of us a promise? He has given us a true friend in Jesus if only we will believe in Him. Jesus is a friend who loves us so much that He died for us. Jonathan didn't break his promise of friendship to David, and you know that Jesus will never break His promise to us—to be our Lord and Savior and our best Friend.

(He exits.)

END PART IV

DAVID: PART V—GLORY

Bible Verse: The LORD will repay each man for his righteousness and his faithfulness *(1 Samuel 26:23).*

(SOLDIERS enter and speak in unison.)

SOLDIERS: We're friends of David.

SOLDIER 1: I sure wish King Saul would quit chasing us.

SOLDIER 2: We ought to just sneak up and *thunk*—that would put an end to all this fuss.

SOLDIER 3: That Saul—he's sure ornery.

NARRATOR: You guessed it. Young David has run away from Saul, who tried to kill him several times. Saul is mad with jealousy. Let's see what happens.

(DAVID enters. SOLDIERS speak together.)

SOLDIERS: David, let's kill Saul so we can all go home. Watcha say, David, can we finish him off? Come on, David.

DAVID: Absolutely not. The Lord made Saul king, and only the Lord can deal with him. We must always do what will glorify God.

SOLDIERS: Awww, man.

DAVID: I hear Saul is on our trail. We'd better hide.

SOLDIER 1: Hide, hide, hide—all we do is hide.

SOLDIER 2: I feel like a mole.

SOLDIER 3: That's nothing. I feel like an ostrich.

DAVID: Let's hide in that cave over there.

(They go into audience. All grumble but DAVID. SAUL enters with sword hidden behind his back.)

SAUL: David, oh, David—come out, come out, wherever you are. I promise you I won't hurt you. *(To audience)* You believe me, don't you? Have you seen David anywhere about? *(Response)*

SAUL: Ah. The Lord smiles on David, but somehow I feel He's always frowning on me. If I could get rid of David, then my son Jonathan could become king, and I could get some peace of mind. Now, I ask you again—have you seen David? *(Response)* You're no help. Hmmmm . . . This looks like a good place to do my calisthenics. 1-2-3-4 . . .

(DAVID *and his men sneak in.*)

SOLDIER 1: Now's our chance.

SOLDIER 2: We'll get him now!

SOLDIER 3: Now Saul is within our power. Get him.

(They start for SAUL, *weapons out.*)

DAVID: Stop! Get back here.

SOLDIERS: Awww, man.

(DAVID *approaches* SAUL *and raises sword.*)

SOLDIER 1: That a boy, David.

SOLDIER 2: He wants to do it himself.

SOLDIER 3: That's why he stopped us.

DAVID *(to audience):* Should I do it? Will killing Saul glorify God? *(Response)* No. May the Lord keep me from doing any harm to my king. The Lord has a plan for my life. I'll let Him work things out.
   (He takes out scissors and cuts a piece of cloth from the robe of SAUL, *who is still doing calisthenics. Then* DAVID *crosses away.*)
   Saul.

SAUL: I know that voice. It's David. Ah-ha!

DAVID: See, I have cut a piece from your garment. I was close enough to kill you, but I didn't. Can't you see that I mean you no harm? You are the king, and I will honor you, and I will always glorify God.

NARRATOR: For a while, Saul didn't hunt for David. He had learned his lesson . . . but after many months passed, Saul once again began to look for David in order to kill him.

(SOLDIERS *enter on tiptoe.*)

SOLDIER 1: Saul is just over that hill. He's sleeping and snoring to beat the band.

SOLDIER 2: Let's go tell David.

(They exit. SAUL *enters sleepwalking, having a nightmare.*)

SAUL: Oh. Spears. Ahhhh. My kingdom is lost. Ohhh. Where is the Lord. Eeeee. Don't leave me. Noooooo! *(Spinning around and waking up)* What a nightmare. So tired from trying to find and kill David. Got to sleep.

(*He lies down and starts to snore.* DAVID *and* SOLDIERS *enter.*)

SOLDIER 1: There he is.

(SOLDIERS *start for* SAUL.)

DAVID: Wait.

SOLDIER 2: God has placed Saul in your hands. Let me get him—one plunge of the old sword, and Saul is no more.

(SOLDIER 2 *crosses and raises sword above* SAUL.)

DAVID: Stop! *(To audience)* Should I let him kill the king? Will that bring glory to God or just to me? *(Response)* No. You must not harm him. I know that the Lord himself will kill Saul—either when his time comes to die a natural death or when he dies in battle. The Lord has a plan for my life and for Saul's. I can't take his life in my hands.

SOLDIERS: Awww, man.

DAVID: I'll take his spear.

(DAVID *takes spear. They leave, then turn back.*)

Saul. King Saul—wake up.

SAUL: What . . . ? David, is that you?

DAVID: Yes, your majesty. Look, here is your spear. I took it from you while you slept. I could have killed you, but I didn't.

SAUL *(sincerely):* I have done wrong. Come back, my son. I will never harm you again. I will give you riches as a reward for sparing my life.

DAVID *(to audience):* Should I go back to him? *(Response)* No, I thank you for the invitation, and I believe you are sincere, but now I can't trust you. And furthermore, my reward comes from the Lord, for the Lord rewards those who are faithful and righteous. Take your spear. I must leave Israel. May God be with you.

(DAVID *and* SOLDIERS *exit.*)

SAUL: That's the problem. God isn't with me.

(Turns back on audience.)

NARRATOR: Saul has disobeyed God. His heart was full of jealousy and hate. Months later, as he was fighting the Philistines, he knew that his time had come, and he died in battle. David and his men were far away when they heard the news.

(DAVID *enters singing a hymn.*)

SOLDIER 1: Have you heard the good news?

SOLDIER 2: Saul is dead.

SOLDIER 3: Now you can be king.

(They celebrate—all but DAVID.*)*

DAVID: Stop. How dare you cheer and shout. Haven't you learned anything? If the Lord wills it, then I will be king. We must not try to build our own kingdoms. We must become part of God's kingdom and let Him do the building. Remember, God has a plan for each of our lives—but they're God's plans, not ours. If I had killed Saul, that would have been my plan—not God's. Now we will not cheer and shout. We will mourn the death of Saul, who was once God's chosen one.

NARRATOR: And you remember, in all our decisions and choices, God has a perfect plan for us, which begins with His making us His own children if we believe in Jesus Christ as our Savior and Lord.

THE END

THE STORY OF ABIGAIL

Bible Verses: 1 Samuel 25

SERVANT: David, David, King Saul continues to search for you. He has even put out a reward for your arrest, and he's heading this way.

DAVID: How many men does he have this time?

SERVANT: A thousand more than us—2,000. But we can set a trap for him. When he goes through the narrow pass, opening onto the Desert of Moan, we'll have our men hurtle down rocks from the cliffs, and he and his men will be smashed like cockroaches. Hee! Hee!

DAVID: No, the Lord will be the Judge of King Saul's actions against me. If I seek revenge, I will be no better than him. We must flee once more.

SERVANT: Flee, flee, flee—I'm tired of fleeing.

DAVID: We will need supplies. For the past several months, we have been protecting the local farmers from bandits and thieves, and we have asked for nothing in return. I hear that Nabal, the richest of these shepherds, is shearing his sheep. Go to him. Greet him in my name and ask if he would provide us with some sheep for our journey.

SERVANT: Oh great! The only thing I hate more than fleeing is message giving. You see, I'm basically a shy person. I avoid strangers whenever possible. I . . .

DAVID: Go! Now!

SERVANT: Right.

(DAVID *and* SERVANT *exit.* NABAL *and* ABIGAIL *enter with* MAIDSERVANT. *For the shearing,* NABAL *could take T-shirt off an actor playing a sheep.)*

NABAL: How many, Abigail?

ABIGAIL: This makes 999 sheep sheared, Nabal.

NABAL: Are you sure you've counted right, wife? I thought I had 1,000.

ABIGAIL: You did. But remember, you promised to donate 1 sheared sheep to the Old Shepherd's Sheep Shearing Retirement Fund.

NABAL: I did what? Impossible. I don't give my sheep to anyone, and I sell all my sheep's wool so that I can stay rich. Where is my sheep now? Where? Where?

ABIGAIL: I gave it to an old shepherd an hour ago.

NABAL: Well, get it back.

ABIGAIL: Nabal, please show a little kindness of heart.

NABAL: Kindness is for weak-hearted wives like yourself. No, get me back my sheep, or I'll shear all the hair from your pretty head. Get! (ABIGAIL *exits.*) Give away my sheep, indeed.

SERVANT *(entering):* Uh, Mr. Nabal, sir . . .

NABAL: Well, speak up, man.

SERVANT: I, uh, er, that is. *(To audience)* I told you I hate delivering messages.

NABAL: What's the matter? Sheep got your tongue? Har! Har!

SERVANT *(reading from scroll):* Greetings from David, the son of Jesse, who has been protecting your sheep from thieves and robbers and who is leaving town and would like to request that you give him some sheep for food, as many as you could spare, anything would be appreciated. Long life and good health to all that is yours. Whew!

NABAL: Long life and good health to all that is mine? You said it, Buster. The key word here is "mine." These sheep belong to me and me alone. They are mine, mine, mine.

SERVANT: All right, forget about the sheep. How about a few loaves of bread then?

NABAL: Get out!

SERVANT: All right, I'm going.

NABAL: The nerve of that guy, asking for my sheep.

(NABAL *exits.* DAVID *and* SERVANT *enter.)*

DAVID: Nabal said what?

SERVANT: He said no, nix, forget it, get lost, and go jump in the lake.

DAVID: Put on your swords, men! I have watched over and protected Nabal and his precious sheep, and now he returns evil for good. Not only will Nabal lose his sheep, but also his life and the lives of his servants. Revenge.

(They exit. NABAL *enters with* MAIDSERVANT.)

NABAL: I want lamb patties for lunch, lamb stew for dinner, and lamb fritters for a bedtime snack. You got that?

ABIGAIL *(enters):* Nabal, Nabal. David is coming with 400 men to take your sheep and destroy your house because you refused to give him even the smallest portion of your wealth.

NABAL (*yawning*): Don't get excited, Abigail. It's all a bluff. He wouldn't dare attack me. He knows if he tried, I'd make shish kabobs of him and his men. Shish kabobs! (*Exiting*) Which reminds me, I'd like lamb shish kabobs for lunch tomorrow, and . . .

(*He leaves.* MAIDSERVANT *follows.* ABIGAIL *brings* MAIDSERVANT *back onstage.*)

ABIGAIL: Quick, get 200 loaves of bread, wine, cakes, and five dressed sheep. Go and present them to David and his men. I will follow. And don't tell Nabal. If he won't save his household, I will.

(ABIGAIL *exits.*)

MAIDSERVANT: Right! I just love delivering messages. I just love it. I'm off. Let's see, that was 50 loaves, 200 sheep, and a partridge in a pear tree.

(*Exits opposite of* ABIGAIL, *writing in notebook.* DAVID *enters with his* SERVANT.)

DAVID: Nabal's house is just down in that valley. Draw your swords, men.

SERVANT: Someone is coming, Sire.

DAVID: It's a woman. Does Nabal send a woman to make peace with me?

ABIGAIL (*enters and bows*): My lord, I am Nabal's wife, Abigail. Let the blame of my husband be upon me. My husband is a fool, and I ask that you not avenge yourself upon him, for the Lord has kept you from bloodshed and revenge in not killing Saul. I ask that you forgive Nabal's greed and let the Lord himself give him due punishment.

DAVID (*aside*): Never have I seen a woman of such wisdom and beauty. (*To* ABIGAIL) Praise be to the Lord who has sent you today to meet me. May you be blessed for keeping me from bloodshed and from avenging with my own hands. You have saved the life of your husband and all his household. Go home in peace.

(*She exits.*)

SERVANT: Aw nuts, I was looking forward to a little bloodshed.

(*They both exit.* NABAL *enters drunk.* MAIDSERVANT *follows.*)

NABAL: Count my money again, my faithful servant. Count my sheep. Count my toes. Count the hairs on my head—they all belong to me.

MAIDSERVANT: Oh good, I just love counting, even though I never seem to get my numbers straight.

ABIGAIL (*enters*): You fool, Nabal. I have just come from David and his 400 soldiers.

NABAL: Huh?

ABIGAIL: Four hundred drawn swords.

NABAL: Gulp!

ABIGAIL: Four hundred drawn swords heading in this direction.

NABAL: Argh!

ABIGAIL: And I gave him sheep and bread and pleaded for your life and the lives of your servants.

(NABAL *goes into paroxysms of dying and falls down dead.* DAVID *enters with* SERVANT.)

DAVID: I have heard of the death of your husband. Through you, the Lord has kept His servant David from wrong doing. Now that this fool is dead, will you come with me and be my wife?

ABIGAIL: Yes. Here is your maidservant, ready to serve you and all your house.

(They exit hand in hand.)

MAIDSERVANT: They make a nice couple, don't you think?

SERVANT: Yes. He's always been a bit headstrong. He could use a bit of Abigail's wisdom even if it does mean less head knocking.

MAIDSERVANT: Well, it looks like we'll be going along with you. I'll miss all these sheep. I just love to count.

SERVANT: Say, you're not married are you?

MAIDSERVANT: You're not suggesting . . . ?

SERVANT: Why not? And I tell you what—we'll have 23 children, and you can run around all day counting and keeping track of them.

MAIDSERVANT: Wait. I just might have something to say about that . . . *(playfully shoving him)*

SERVANT: I'd be happy with five: two boys, three girls . . . but no sheep!

(They exit hand in hand.)

THE END

THE STORY OF ESTHER: PART I

(XERXES *enters, kingly regalia. With him is* HAMAN.)

XERXES: My name is Xerxes—that's King Xerxes to you—king of all Persia. When I snap my fingers, people jump.
> *(He snaps his fingers.* HAMAN, *who is standing next to him, jumps.)*
> See? When I speak, people run to do my commands. Get me grapes, servant.
> *(*HAMAN *snaps fingers.* SERVANT *jumps, runs in with grapes.)*
> I've got an itch.
> *(*HAMAN *snaps fingers,* SERVANT *jumps and runs on with scratcher.)*
> A little more to the left. Ahhh! Send me Queen Vashti.

(HAMAN *snaps fingers,* SERVANT *jumps, runs off.* VASHTI'S *voice is heard offstage.)*

VASHTI: Tell Xerxy the Jersky that I'm in the middle of my beauty treatment and that I can't be bothered.

(SERVANT *runs on.)*

SERVANT: She won't, gulp, come, Sire.

XERXES: What? How dare she disobey my royal command. I'll snap my royal fingers myself this time. Haman . . . *(Snaps fingers.* HAMAN *and* SERVANT *jump.)* Tell Queen Vashti to get out here by the count of three.

HAMAN: Do it.

(Snaps fingers. SERVANT *jumps and exits.)*

XERXES: One

VASHTI *(voice is heard offstage):* Tell Xerxy the Jersky that I'm getting my hair done.

XERXES: Two . . .

SERVANT: She refuses to come, oh Sire.

XERXES: Three! Now she's done it. How dare she disobey my royal command. I'll . . . I'll . . . what would you do if you were me, Haman?

HAMAN: I'd banish Vashti from my presence, Sire. Then I'd have a contest among the most beautiful young women in the land and pick myself a new queen.

XERXES: Let it be done. And also make a proclamation that every man should be ruler of his own household.

(*He snaps his fingers, HAMAN jumps and exits. All exit. MORDECAI enters wringing his hands.*)

MORDECAI: Oy-vey, just look at me, I'm a nervous wreck. I always wring my hands like this when I'm a nervous wreck. I can't stop. My name is Mordecai. I'm a Jew who lives in the land of Persia, and I have just received official notification that my beautiful adopted daughter Esther must appear before the king.

(*ESTHER enters. She has a suitcase with her.*)

ESTHER: Mordecai, please don't worry. Stop wringing your hands like that.

MORDECAI: All right, already. I'll stop.

(*He starts biting his nails.*)

ESTHER: My dear, dear father. Stop biting your nails. (*He goes back to wringing his hands.*) I'll be all right. The king will never pick me anyway.

MORDECAI: But what if he does? And what if he finds out you are Jewish, and you can't eat pork and things, and . . .

ESTHER: And that I worship the one true God, Jehovah?

MORDECAI: Especially that! You must not tell him that you are a Jew, because we cannot bow down to any man or any god but the one true God.

ESTHER: But Mordecai, it is our God who has promised to watch over us and to protect us if we obey Him.

MORDECAI: I know, I know . . . just say nothing, all right?

ESTHER: All right, I promise—if you will stop wringing your hands.

MORDECAI: There, I've stopped.

ESTHER: Good-bye, Mordecai. Don't worry.

MORDECAI: Yes, yes, and don't forget to send me a postcard.

(*She kisses him on the cheek and exits. He struggles for a moment and then begins to wring his hands.*)
    Oy-vey, and woe is me.
(*A beauty pageant. HAMAN is officiating. In background, Miss America theme song is hummed or sung. The first two contestants should look pretty brutish. Could be played by guys.*)

HAMAN: And now for the final three contestants. Here we have Miss Mesopotamia. Isn't she a beauty folks?

MISS M: I'd just like to say that polka dot is my favorite color, and I ride camels for a hobby.

HAMAN: And next we have Miss Hilda Hittite.

MISS H: I eat old cigars for lunch and skin camels for a living, and I'm into self-defense. Hi-yaaa.

HAMAN: And last of all, from . . . from . . . *(To* SERVANT.*)* Where is she from, Blurb?

SERVANT: Just outside the city gates.

HAMAN: Hmmm, yes. Miss Esther, one of our local beauties. *(To* SERVANT, *aside)* She's not one of those Israelites. Is she from the Jewish settlement?

*(*SERVANT *shrugs.)*

XERXES: Oh my, it's so hard for me to make up my mind. *(To audience)* Could you help me? All who think I should make Miss Mesopotamia my queen clap loudly and cheer. How about Hilda the Hittite? Well, what about Esther? *(Loud response)* I was hoping you'd say that. Let it hereby be proclaimed that Esther will be my new queen. Boy, are we going to have a party tonight. *(Exits with* ESTHER.*)*

HAMAN: Hmmm. Something fishy is going on here. *(To* SERVANT*)* Let's go nose around the Jewish quarter of town and see if we can find out more about this Esther lady.

(They circle around and come upon MORDECAI *in the street standing and praying.)*

MORDECAI *(aside to audience):* What should I do? If I bow down, he'll leave me and all my other Jewish neighbors alone, but that would be disobeying my Lord, the one true God. But if I don't bow down, Haman will take this . . . *(Hits head)* . . . from this. *(Hits chest)* How many of you would bow down? How many of you would not bow down? *(Response)* OK, gulp, here goes. *(To* HAMAN*)* The law that our God has given us forbids us to bow down to any god or any man but the one true God. Therefore, I cannot bow down to you.

HAMAN: You dog, you cat, you lumpish frog—you and all your people will pay for this.

(He exits.)

MORDECAI: Now what have I done? What was it that Esther said?

ESTHER *(offstage):* But Mordecai, it is our God who has promised to watch over and protect us.

MORDECAI: Well, I obeyed Him, but I don't feel very protected right now. Would you all wring your hands with me? There, that makes me feel better. And will you bite your nails with me. Oh, that's nice. I'm afraid I've gotten everybody into a lot of trouble. What will Haman do to all our people?

NARRATOR: Come back next time for the conclusion of the exciting adventure of Esther.

(He exits.)

END PART I

THE STORY OF ESTHER: PART II

(MORDECAI *enters, wringing his hands.*)

MORDECAI: If you remember what happened yesterday, the king's evil adviser, Haman, became enraged with me when I refused to bow down to him. Now my people are in trouble. What will he do? Esther told me that those who love and obey the one true God, why, He will then protect them. Do you think that is true? I wonder what Haman is telling the king right now.

(*He exits.* XERXES *enters with a hoe or shovel.* HAMAN *enters a bit later.*)

XERXES: I love to garden. Someday I'll plant a huge garden in Babylon. I know! It will be a hanging garden, and it'll be one of the wonders of the world.

HAMAN: My Lord, there are certain people whose customs are different than ours and who refuse to obey our laws.

XERXES: Hmmm. Yes. Do you think the rhododendrons should go over here or over there?

HAMAN: If it please the King, let a decree be issued to destroy them.

XERXES: My rhododendrons?

HAMAN: No. The Jewish people. Wherever they are in the nation, let them be driven out. (*Pause*) I think they should go over there.

XERXES: Yes. Now, what were you saying?

HAMAN: These troublesome people . . .

XERXES: Yes, yes, do with them as you please. (HAMAN *exits.*) Now, what about the clematis?

(*He exits.* MORDECAI *enters.*)

MORDECAI: Oh me, oh my. I'm rubbing my hands to the bone.

(*He overhears two suspicious looking people.*)

MAN 1: Let's kill the king today, mate.

MAN 2: Why not? Good day for a killing. He will be working in his garden and all, an easy mark. We'll clobber him with his spade.

MAN 1: And bury him in the tulips.

MORDECAI: What? Ho! Two murderers plotting the death of the king. Arrest them.

MAN 2: Keep your voice down would you, mate?

MORDECAI: You're not going anyplace.
> *(They try to escape. He hits them on their heads and drags them off.)*
> To the king's officer with both of you.

(HAMAN and SERVANT enter. An actor plays the scaffold holding a rope that looks like a noose.)

HAMAN: Put it up over there. You see that? A scaffold 70 feet tall, and the first to hang from it will be Mordecai the Jew because he wouldn't bow down to me. So just as the king commanded me, I've arrested him and all his people in order to hang them by the neck until they're dead, dead, dead.

(MORDECAI enters with XERXES and ESTHER.)

HAMAN: There he is, arrest him.
> *(SERVANT grabs MORDECAI and puts rope around his neck.)*
> Any last words?

XERXES: What's going on here?

HAMAN: I'll tell you what's going on. This here is Mordecai the Jew, a trouble-maker if I've ever seen one. He's the one who wouldn't bow down to me, so just as you commanded me, I've arrested him and all his people in order to hang them by the neck until they're dead, dead, dead.

XERXES: Did I make such a decree? I don't remember.

MORDECAI: Esther, help. Do something. Save me. Save our people.

ESTHER: King Xerxes, if you are going to hang this man, then you must hang me too, because I am a Jew like him.

HAMAN: Just as I figured. Get in line; you're next. Hang both of them.

XERXES: Wait a minute. This man here, who saved my life from two murderers, and this, my queen, whom I love more than any creature on earth, are both Jews?

ESTHER AND HAMAN: Yes.

MORDECAI: And our only crime, if crime it be, is that we believe in the one true God.

XERXES: Is this true, Esther?

ESTHER: My king and my husband, you know that I love you dearly, but I love my Lord the one true God even more.

(Pause)

XERXES: I can live with that.

ESTHER: But your adviser here, Haman, loves only himself, so . . .

XERXES: So, let him hang from the scaffold he had made for others.

(The rope is put around HAMAN's neck, and he is taken offstage screaming.)

ESTHER: And what about my people?

XERXES: I hereby make another decree that all the Jews in Persia be allowed to live peacefully and to defend themselves. Are you coming?

ESTHER: In a minute, my King. (XERXES *exits.)* Look, Mordecai, your hands have stopped wringing.

MORDECAI: You're right. I don't believe it.

ESTHER: Our Lord always watches over us. Do you think it was just an accident that I happened to be picked over all the women in the kingdom to be the king's wife, or that it was just an accident that you overheard those two murderers plotting the death of the king?

MORDECAI: No. I guess not.

ESTHER: So stop worrying, and remember—if we love and obey our Lord, He will always watch over us and take care of us.

MORDECAI: Yes, you're probably right.

(He starts wringing his hands.)

ESTHER: What now?

MORDECAI: The lentil soup. I left it on the fire. It's probably burnt to a crisp. Or worse, it's on fire, maybe the house is on fire, maybe the whole block is . . . ahhhh!

(He runs off. ESTHER laughs, shrugs, and exits.)

THE END

DANIEL: PART I—DANIEL AND HIS FRIENDS

NARRATOR: This is the story of Daniel and his friends and the many adventures that they experienced in a strange and foreign land. How many of you have ever been taken from your house and made to march hundreds of miles to another country? Well, that is what happened to Daniel. You see, Daniel was an Israelite, and he lived in Jerusalem. But God was very displeased with the Israelites—they worshiped strange idols, they broke the Ten Commandments, and they didn't love Him or their neighbors very much at all. So He allowed King Nebuchadnezzar of Babylon to take the city and the country with his armies and to make slaves of the Israelites. Look, here come some of the Israeli slaves now, and they don't look very happy.

(Grumbling noises from SLAVES as they enter.)

SLAVE 1: My feet are killing me. *(Grumbles)*

SLAVE 2: Do you think we'll ever see Jerusalem again?

SLAVE 3: Babylon or bust! If I don't get some rest soon, I'm going to be the one that's busted. *(Grumbles)*

SLAVE 1: Do you think God could be here too?

SLAVE 2: No way, God could never be in such a terrible place as this!

(Sound of trumpet)

SLAVE 1: Quiet. Here comes the king, Nebuchadnezzar, and his chief official, Ashpenaz.

(ASHPENAZ and KING N enter.)

ASHPENAZ: Bow before the King.

(SLAVES bow.)

KING N: Ashpenaz, I want you to select for me the most intelligent, the most good-looking, and most agreeable slaves from the 10,000 Jewish slaves before me. Once you have selected them, take them to my royal court, and they will be trained to serve me and to offer me advice. They will eat the same food and drink the same wine as we do. We will make good little Babylonians out of them.

ASHPENAZ: You, come over here.

SLAVE 1: Yes, sir, I can sing and dance. Why I was made for your royal court, Sire. *(Sings, "She'll be coming around the mountain when she comes . . .")*

ASHPENAZ: Send him to the salt mines. Next.

(SLAVE 1 exits.)

SLAVE 2: Me? You picked yourself a winner, my lord. Why, I know more jokes than you can snap your fingers at. I'll keep your royal court in stitches. Did you ever hear the one about . . .

ASHPENAZ: Send him to the pig sties. Next.

(SLAVE 2 exits.)

SLAVE 3: Why, my lord, fancy that you should select little ol' me. Why, I'd make a wonderful addition to your courtsy wortsy. I'm not much good at singing or tellin' jokes, but I'm a wonderful gossip. Why, in two weeks, I'll know every little nasty detail about everyone in your court, and believe me, I can't keep a secret. Why, did you know that . . .

ASHPENAZ: Send her to the barnyard where she can cluck to the hens.

(SLAVE 3 exits.)

KING N: Is this the best you can do, Ashpenaz?

ASHPENAZ *(calls out):* Daniel, Shadrach, come up here. *(They enter.)* Sire, here are Daniel and Shadrach, two slaves; but they come from good families, and they are very intelligent.

KING N: Um, they'll do. . . . Start their training immediately, and be sure that you feed them well. I don't want to be surrounded by any scrawny slaves.

ASHPENAZ: Yes sir. (KING N *exits.)* All right, you two, get to the royal palace, and be sure to keep your bellies full. You heard the king.

(He exits.)

SHADRACH: Well, Daniel, we certainly are lucky to have been picked to be trained for the king's royal court. Our Jewish brothers and sisters will sweat in the fields or dig in the mines. We shall have fine clothes and all the food we can eat.

DANIEL: Yes, Shadrach, we are fortunate. We will serve the king, but we must remember that no matter what happens we must serve our Lord first. He is not only a God in Israel. He is here too, and I don't intend to do anything that might not please our God.

SHADRACH: You are right, Daniel. We must be careful.

(They exit.)

NARRATOR: The next morning, the people came to present food to the idol that they worshiped.

(*A large idol appears.* PEOPLE *dance around it offering it wine and food, chanting things such as, "Here, O Idol, put your blessing on our food." "Here, O Idol, have some Grape-Nuts," etc. They exit, all except idol.*)

SHADRACH: Look, Daniel, they are offering food to the idol before they eat it.

DANIEL: Yes, I see. Shadrach, we mustn't eat the meat or drink the wine that they have offered to the idol, for the Lord our God has taught us that we must not worship any idols. Eating that food would be like worshiping their false god.

(ASHPENAZ *enters.*)

ASHPENAZ: All right you two, here's some meat and some tasty wine, so eat and drink up. No scrawny servants—you heard the king.

SHADRACH: What will we do, Daniel? He wants us to eat the food that has been offered to that idol. I suppose it would be OK. . . . After all, our God probably isn't here anyway. He probably stayed back in Israel.

DANIEL: Not so, Shadrach—our God is the one and only true God. And He is everywhere—in Israel, in Babylon, and throughout the entire universe! Trust in the Lord our God, Shadrach. He will see us through. Ashpenaz, we serve the Lord our God, the one true God. We cannot eat the meat or drink the wine that has been offered to your idol, for that would be a sin. Let us eat only vegetables and drink only water.

ASHPENAZ: No, never. You can't get fat on vegetables and water. And besides, the king decides what you shall eat and drink, and if you don't look as fit as the other young men, the king may kill me. You may want to sacrifice your stomachs, but I don't want to sacrifice my neck.

DANIEL: Test us for 10 days only. For 10 days feed us only vegetables and water. Then compare us with the young men who are eating the food that has been sacrificed to the idol.

SHADRACH: Yes, 10 days, that is all we ask.

ASHPENAZ: Ten days? Oh, all right. But not a second more. But you are both fools. No one can get fat on vegetables and water—yuck! Remember, 10 days. (*Exits*)

DANIEL: What's your favorite vegetable, Shadrach?

SHADRACH: Lima beans—I hear they're fattening.

DANIEL: Trust in the Lord, Shadrach. He is here, and He will see us through. Let's go. (*Exits*)

NARRATOR: What will happen to our young Israeli slaves? If they are weak or have lost weight, they will be ordered to eat food. And, if they refuse to eat the food, they will be put to death for sure. Ten days have passed. Here come Shadrach and Daniel now. Will they be strong? *(Exits)*

(SHADRACH *and* DANIEL *enter.)*

SHADRACH: One potato, two potato, three potato, four . . . you know, Daniel, eating only vegetables isn't as bad as I thought.

DANIEL: When you are serving the Lord, just about anything can taste good. Look, here comes Ashpenaz now.

(ASHPENAZ *enters.)*

ASHPENAZ: Nine days, 23 hours, 59 seconds—10 days. OK, your time is up. I'll bet I'll have to fatten you two up on some idol burgers and some idol cola. Stand over here. Hm . . . teeth look all right, arms are strong, yes . . . ah . . . you two look great. Yes, your God has looked after you. You look even healthier than the other young slaves of the court. I will tell the king that you are getting on well. Oh, and by the way, you can keep eating vegetables if you like. You sure you wouldn't want an idol burger?

DANIEL: No thanks.

SHADRACH: You know, Daniel, the Lord sure watches over those who love and obey His commandments. I thought He only watched over people in Israel, but now I've learned that He is everywhere . . . that He is even *here!*

DANIEL: You are right, Shadrach. Let's tell Him how grateful we are by praying to Him.
      Dear Lord, thank You for being everywhere and especially for being *here* with us all the time. Thanks for watching over us and for helping us to do what is right. Amen.
      Well, Shadrach, it's time for dinner, what's on the menu for tonight?

SHADRACH: Beet burgers and carrot cola.

DANIEL: Good, let's go.

(They exit.)

NARRATOR: And so Daniel and his friends learned that God is everywhere . . . even *here.* For the next three years they studied until they became the king's most trusted advisers. Be sure to come back next time when Daniel's friends have to make a very important decision about who is holy. How will they survive in this strange land? Will they be faithful to God? Come back next time to hear about faith versus the furnace. *(Exits)*

END PART I

DANIEL: PART II— MESHACH, SHADRACH, AND ABEDNEGO

KING N: Heave ho! Heave ho! Come on, come on, you lazy, good-for-nothing slaves. Can't you go any faster? (*Slowly the great statue of the idol ascends.*) Oh, isn't it beautiful? I, King Nebuchadnezzar, have erected the largest and most magnificent statue in all the known countries of the earth. Look at it shine. It's made of gold. And do you know the best thing about this statue? It resembles me. Look at that beard. Look at those intelligent yet loving eyes. Look at that firm, erect body. Oh how I love you, great golden statue. (*Starts kissing the statue*)

Hey, Herald! Get out here, I want you to take down an announcement.

(*He whispers in* HERALD's *ear.* HERALD *reads scroll.*)

HERALD: Hear ye! Hear ye! By order of King Nebuchadnezzeddezetersp, er.... Nebucsuffergater . . . I never could say that name . . . By order of his majesty, the king. All important people in the kingdom of Babylon and outlying provinces are to come and bow down to this mighty statue— which just happens to look a little like the king himself—and worship it. When you hear the sound of the mighty trumpet, everyone—and the king means everyone—is to bow down before that image. And here comes the best part—if anyone doesn't bow down before this idol, they will be cast into the fiery furnace, and they will be burned to death. Hee! Hee!

(KING N *and the* HERALD *exit.* NUB *enters with* NIB.)

NUB: Hey Nib.

NIB: What's on your mind, Nub? Those garden slugs I had for dinner didn't settle very well, and I ain't in the mood for any of yer wild schemes.

NUB: Now's our chance to get back at those three Jewish kids, Meshach, Shadrach, and Abednego, for winning the king's favor while we end up cleaning the king's stables. Them foreigners has been too uppity lately.

NIB: Oh, I don't know, Nub. I like the sound of their names anyway. It's fun to dance to . . .

(*He dances about singing "Meshach, Shadrach, and Abednego," etc.*)

NUB: Can it! Are you some kinda nut or something? Don't you see, this statue is just the thing we've been looking for . . .

NIB: Why's that, Nub? We gonna push it over on them? It looks kinda heavy to do that.

NUB: You nitwit, Nib. The king says that everyone—and he means everyone—is supposed to bow down to that statue and worship it. Well, Meshach, Shadrach, and Abednego love their God, and they will refuse to bow down to this statue. Then can you guess what will happen?

NIB: Err, let me see. They won't bow down, and then they won't get backaches, and they will be a lot healthier than the rest of us.

NUB: No, you dimwit. They will be thrown into the fiery furnace, and then we shall be rid of them. Hee! Hee! Look, here they come now. Hide behind the statue—quick!

(Three friends enter.)

MESHACH: Look, there it is. There's the statue.

SHADRACH: It is big, Meshach. What should we do, Abednego?

ABEDNEGO: Well, we can't bow down to it, that's for sure. Why don't we take a vacation so when they sound the trumpet, we will be long gone?

MESHACH: We are still slaves, Abednego. We might be the King's advisers, but I'm sure he's not going to let us run off on some vacation. No, we'll have to stay, and stay standing too—even if it costs us our lives. We can't bow down to false idols. Only God is holy! This is just a big hunk of stone. Bowing to it would be breaking the law of our Lord.

SHADRACH: Let's go get some sleep. Something tells me that tomorrow is going to be a rough day.

(They exit.)

NUB: Did you hear that, Nib? . . . Nib? Wake up!

NIB: Awww! I was dreaming of mashed potatoes and southern fried chicken—why did you have to wake me up?

NUB: Didn't you hear what they said, Nib? They don't plan to bow down to the statue when the trumpet blows tomorrow. They've cooked their goose for sure. Let's go tell the king.

(They exit.)

NARRATOR: The next day, all the important people had gathered before the statue of the king, and the trumpet was about to blow.

(NIB *and* NUB *enter to stand before* KING N)

KING N: But what you say can't be true, Nub. Meshach, Shadrach, and Abednego are three of my very best advisers. They will bow down to the statue. You will see. Blow the trumpet.

(Sound of trumpet being blown. The three friends enter.)

MESHACH: All right, friends, the trumpet has blown; stand firm and don't bow to that idol.

NIB: Look, your majesty, the three Jewish advisers, they are not bowing to the statue, just as I said.

KING N: What? Can this be true? My friends, have you lost your hearing? The trumpet has blown, and you are to bow down to my statue and worship it. If you do not worship this statue, you will be cast into the fiery furnace. I'll give you one more chance. Blow the trumpet again.
(The trumpet sounds. All bow except for the three.)
There, you've done it. You've disobeyed me and insulted me, and you shall die for it, and who is the God that will deliver you out of my hands?

SHADRACH: O Nebuchadnezzar, we have no need to answer you in this matter. Only the Lord our God is holy and worthy to be worshiped. Our God is able to save us from the burning, fiery furnace, and He will save us from your hand, King. But even if He does not deliver us, we will not serve your gods or worship the golden image that you have set up.

(Fiery furnace can be made by using red crepe-paper streamers.)

KING N: You, you . . . make the furnace seven times hotter . . . and you, you there, throw them in so that they are burned to a cinder, the insolent pups. What? What's this? Why the fire is so fierce that it consumed the soldier who was throwing them in. Oh, I can't look, they must be turned to smoke by now. You, you out there. *(To audience)* You tell me when they are burned to a crisp so that I can turn the fire down. Are they dead yet? What? They aren't? But what is this I see? I see four men, not three, walking in the midst of the fire; and look—they are not hurt. The fire hasn't hurt them at all! And . . . and look! Why the appearance of the fourth is like a son of the gods. Bring Shadrach, Meshach, and Abednego to me. *(They come from the fire.)* Blessed be the God of Meshach, Shadrach, and Abednego, who has sent His angel to deliver His servants who have trusted in Him. Truly He is a great God, and I shall make a decree: Anybody that speaks anything against the God of Shadrach, Meshach, and Abednego shall be condemned, for truly their God is holy. And there is no other god who is able to deliver in this way. Come, my friends, we will have a celebration.

(Cast exits celebrating.)

NARRATOR: The very same God that rescued Meshach, Shadrach, and Abednego is the God of you and the God of all of us. Yes, they worshiped and trusted in the one true God, and He rescued them from the fiery furnace. Only He is holy and worthy to be praised and worshiped. So trust in Him, and you shall be saved. *(Exit)*

END PART II

DANIEL: PART III— THE TREE

NARRATOR: In today's story, we find King Nebuchadnezzar at home in his palace, contented and prosperous.
(KING N *comes in all happy and stretches to take a nap.*)
But he had a dream that terrified him.
(*We see* KING N *having his dream.*)
So, as always, he had his magicians, enchanters, astrologers, and diviners brought before him and told them the dream, but they could not interpret it for him. Finally he got wise and called Daniel.

KING N: Daniel! Daniel, where are you?

DANIEL (*enters*): I am here, your majesty. What can I do for you?

KING N: I have had a very disturbing dream, and I know that the spirit of the holy gods is in you and there is no mystery too difficult for you.

DANIEL: Tell me your dream, and with God's help, I will tell you the meaning.

KING N: This is the dream. . . . I looked, and right in front of me stood a tree in the middle of the land.

(*A person dressed as a tree comes in with large branches. Also, children can become animals and birds beneath the tree.*)

It was incredibly tall, and it grew large and strong, and its top touched the sky. It had beautiful leaves and lots and lots of fruit and food for everyone. Underneath it, the animals found shade, and the birds lived in its branches. From it every creature was fed. Then a messenger from heaven came down and said . . .

MESSENGER: Cut down the tree and trim off its branches; strip off its leaves and scatter its fruit. Let the animals run away from under it, and let the birds fly away from its branches. But let the stump and its roots, bound with iron and bronze, remain in the ground in the grass of the field. (*All these things are done.*) This stump, it is like a great man full of pride. Let him live out in the rain and dew and live with the animals and plants of the earth. Let his mind be changed from that of a man, and let him be given the mind of an animal for seven years. This message is given so that everyone can know that God is the King over all kingdoms and gives kingdoms to whomever He wishes.

KING N: Now, Daniel, tell me the meaning of this dream.

NARRATOR: Daniel was worried about the meaning of the dream, but Nebuchadnezzar told him . . .

KING N: Do not let the dream or its meaning worry you. Just tell me the true meaning of the dream.

DANIEL: Oh, King, if only this dream was meant for someone else, for you see, you are that tree. For you have become strong, and your greatness has grown until it reaches the sky. But you will be driven away from people and will live with the wild animals; you will eat grass like cattle and be drenched with rain from heaven. Seven years will pass by until you finally realize and admit that the most high God is truly the King of all kings and that He is more powerful than you are. Then when you admit that God is Ruler of all, you will once again become the king.

(KING N *is abashed, looks fearfully around.* DANIEL *exits.*)

NARRATOR: All of this happened to the king just as Daniel had said. Twelve months after the dream, the king was walking up on the roof of his royal palace and admiring all that he had made.

KING N: Look at all the great things I have done and all the great buildings I have built with all my power for my glory!

NARRATOR: Right after he said these words, a voice from heaven said . . .

VOICE: This is what is decreed for you, King Nebuchadnezzar: Your royal authority has been taken from you. You will be driven away from people and will live with the wild animals. You will eat grass like cattle until you finally realize that only God most high is the true King of kings and He is the one who makes all of these kingdoms possible.

NARRATOR: Then the king was driven away and went crazy. He ate grass with the cattle.

(COWS *enter.*)

COW 1: Moo! Isn't that the king?

COW 2: Yeah, he likes the alfalfa hay.

COW 1: Why is he out here with us?

COW 2: Because he thinks he's as good as God.

COW 1: Hello! I'm only a dumb cow, and I know better than that!

NARRATOR: And he was drenched with rain.
(KING *is wetted down with watering can by* NARRATOR.)
Finally, after seven years, he came back to his senses and realized that God, the Most High, was the only one worthy of our praise.

KING N: Oh, God, please forgive me. . . . Now I realize that You and only You are the King of all kings and that You give kingdoms to those You wish and take kingdoms from others. You are here and everywhere. . . . You alone are holy! You are the Savior, and now, God, please be forgiving!

NARRATOR: At that same time, the king became normal again and was not crazy anymore. He returned to his kingdom.

KING N: Listen to me, everyone! Praise and exalt the King of heaven, God the Most High, because only He is worthy to be praised and He is a forgiving God, if we turn back to Him and repent of our sins.

NARRATOR: Just as God forgave Nebuchadnezzar once he turned from his sin, so He will forgive us through Jesus Christ. Our God is a forgiving God!

(Exit.)

END PART III

DANIEL: PART IV— NEBUCHADNEZZAR'S DREAM—PRAISE GOD

(Music in the background)

NARRATOR: This week, we have learned a good deal about God through our dramas about Daniel. But I never told you how Daniel became the chief adviser of King Nebuchadnezzar . . . did I? Well, it went this way: Night had descended over the city of Babylon. All its inhabitants slept quietly . . . *(Sound of snoring)* . . . except for one man, the king himself, Nebuchadnezzar. He was having a terrifying dream. Have you ever had nightmares? They certainly can be frightening, can't they? *(A scream comes from KING N.)* Oh, but let's hear what King Nebuchadnezzar is dreaming about.

KING N: Oh, no . . . no, don't smash me . . . no, here it comes . . . ahhhh! *(Wakes)* Oh, what a dream. I've never been so frightened in my life. Look at me sweat. That was the worst dream I've ever had. It must be a very important dream. Yes, it was sent by the gods to warn me about something. I must find out what it meant. *(To audience)* Maybe you can help me. You see, in this dream I . . . that is, well, it went like this . . . um, that's funny, I can't seem to remember what the dream was about. In fact, I've forgotten it entirely. This is terrible. The most important dream of my life, and I can't remember what it is. I know, I'll call my chief wise man. Hey, wise man!

(WISE MAN enters wearing graduation hat.)

WISE MAN: Oh bother, waking me in the middle of the night. I need my rest, you know—keeps my wise brain from withering up. You called, Sire?

KING N: I'm very worried about a dream I've had. I want to know what it means.

WISE MAN *(to audience):* This should be easy enough. He tells me the dream, and I tell him what it means. I can make up anything I like, and he'll never know the difference. Then I can get back to my nice goose-feather bed and downy pillow to rest my wise head. *(To KING)* Well, Sire, I am waiting. Tell me the dream so that I can tell you what it means.

KING N: But you don't understand. I can't remember the dream. You have to tell me what I dreamed and what it all means. Now be quick. After all, you are the wisest of the wise men—get on with it.

WISE MAN (*to audience*): Did he say what I thought he said? No, it couldn't be. (*Laughs nervously*) Now, if you will but tell me the dream, I will be more than happy to tell you what it means.

KING N: If you don't tell me my dream and its meaning, I will have you torn limb from limb and make your house a garbage heap. But if you can tell me both the dream and its meaning, I will reward you with gifts and great honor. Speak up.

WISE MAN (*to audience*): He's serious, isn't he? (*To* KING) Sire, there is no one on the face of the earth who can tell you the dream.

KING N: Enough of this. You are only trying to gain time. You are slow and cowardly—you are a stupid wise man. Send in the captain of the guard.

(CAPTAIN *enters marching out loud.*)

CAPTAIN: Captain of the guard at your service, Sire.

KING N: Take him away.

WISE MAN: But Sire, what your majesty is asking for is so difficult that no one can do it for you except the gods, and they do not live among human beings.

KING N: Excuses, excuses. Guard, round up all the wise men in the country and execute them—cut off their heads, and then we'll see how wise they are. Oh, yes, and make their houses into garbage heaps while you're at it.

CAPTAIN: Come on, move.

(CAPTAIN *and* WISE MAN *exit.*)

KING N: Isn't there anyone who can tell me my dream?

(NARRATOR *enters along with* DANIEL *and the* CAPTAIN.)

NARRATOR: The king had issued the orders. All the wise men, including Daniel, had been arrested and were about to be killed.

(*A sword is raised above* DANIEL's *head by the* CAPTAIN.)

DANIEL: Wait. Why are you doing this?

CAPTAIN: I don't know for sure. Something about the king and a dream and telling him what it means. Mine's not to reason why; mine's just to see all you guys die.

DANIEL: Listen to me. Take me to the king. I will tell the king the meaning of his dream. I can save you the trouble of having to kill all these wise men.

CAPTAIN: Aye, all those heads being chopped off would make a big mess, and you can bet your boots that I'd be the one to have to clean it up. I suppose it won't hurt. Come along.

(They exit.)

NARRATOR: And so Daniel was taken before the king himself.

KING N: Isn't there anyone who can tell me my dream?

(DANIEL enters with CAPTAIN.)

CAPTAIN: Excuse me, Sire, this fellow here says he can tell you your dream.

DANIEL: No, Sire, I can't tell you your dream . . .

KING N: What! Then why are you wasting my time? Off with his head.

DANIEL: But . . . there is a God in heaven who reveals all mysteries. Give me tonight so that He can reveal the dream and its meaning to me. That is all I ask.

KING N: Umph! Well, all right . . . but, if in the morning you can't tell me the dream, then you will be the first to die.

(They exit.)

NARRATOR: That night, Daniel prayed to God to reveal to him the dream and its meaning.

DANIEL: O God, who knows all things and who is wiser than all men, reveal the secrets of this dream to me. Ah, . . . I see . . . yes . . . to be sure. I praise You, Lord, and thank You for telling me the meaning of this dream.

NARRATOR: And so Daniel returned to tell the king the meaning of his dream.

KING N: So, Daniel, you have had your one night. Now let us see if you can tell what nobody else can. What is the meaning of my dream?

DANIEL: My Lord has told me that while your majesty was sleeping, you dreamed about the future, and God, who reveals mysteries, showed you what is going to happen. This is what you saw: You saw standing before you a giant statue—its head was made of gold, its chest and arms were made of silver, its legs of iron, and its feet of clay. But as you watched, a stone broke loose from a cliff without anyone touching it, and struck and shattered the statue. Soon the stone grew to be a mountain that covered the whole earth.

(In background, cardboard cutouts can mime this story.)

KING N: Yes, yes, now I remember. But what does it mean?

DANIEL: Now I will tell you. You, my king, are the head of gold. God has given you power and wealth and wisdom. The head stands for you, King Nebuchadnezzar and for the kingdom of Babylon, and the other parts of the body stand for other great empires. The stone stands for the kingdom of God, which will come in the future and which will destroy all the other kingdoms. God's kingdom will come, and it will go on forever.

KING N: It is not a happy dream for me, but it is the truth. Daniel, your God is the greatest of all gods. I know this because you have been able to explain my dream. Now, I will make you chief adviser over all my advisers and will give you many splendid gifts. And we should praise this God who is setting up an everlasting kingdom.

(They exit.)

NARRATOR: Yes, this same God, who is everywhere and even here all the time, who is holy and who is our Savior and who is forgiving, is truly worthy to be praised. *(Exits)*

END PART IV

DANIEL: PART V— DANIEL AND THE LIONS

Bible Verse: The salvation of the righteous is from the LORD; He is their strength in time of trouble. And the LORD helps them, and delivers them . . . because they take refuge in Him *(Psalm 37:39-40)*.

NARRATOR: Today, we are going to act out a story with animals in it. OK, let's show the kids what kind of animals we will be in this story.
  (Actors become monkeys. NARRATOR gets mad.)
  Not monkeys. *(Whispers with actors.)* That's right! See if you can guess now what animals are in the story. *(Actors become lions.)*
  Lions—you're right.

DANIEL SONG
Daniel, Daniel, Daniel boy,
Why are you jumping high for joy?
Can't you feel those lions bite?
They give me a terrible fright.
Daniel prays 'cause he loves his mighty Lord.
Daniel, Daniel, Daniel boy,
Why are you jumping high for joy?
Can't you hear those lions roar?
They just locked the dungeon door.
Daniel prays 'cause he loves his mighty Lord.
Daniel, Daniel, Daniel boy,
Why are you jumping high for joy?
Can't you see those lion paws?
With their sharp and deadly claws?
Daniel prays 'cause he loves his mighty Lord.

NARRATOR: Yes, this is the story of Daniel and the Lions. Daniel loved his Lord more than anything on earth. And do you know how Daniel told the Lord of his love?
  (DANIEL comes out and kneels down to pray.)
  That's right, he prayed to Him—morning, noon, and night.

(One cast member runs across with "morning" sign.)

DANIEL: Praise You, Lord. I thank You for that good night's rest. *(Runner with "afternoon" sign)* I praise You, Lord, for guiding me through the morning with Your blessing. *(Runner with "evening" sign)* Good-night, Lord, let even my dreams be about my love for You.

NARRATOR: But Daniel lived as a captive under King Darius in a land that was far away from Jerusalem. He was a slave, but the Lord had blessed Daniel with great spirit and great wisdom so that King Darius made him one of his closest advisers. Of course, this made the king's other advisers very mad.

KING D: Tell me, Daniel, what should we do with the crops this year?

DANIEL: Store the wheat, and you will have nothing to fear.

(Other ADVISERS *growl jealously.)*

KING D: Tell me, Daniel, what should we do about our enemies?

DANIEL: Attack with our navy first and then with our armies.

(ADVISERS *growl noisily.)*

KING D: Tell me, Daniel, what should we do about the noise in this place?

DANIEL: Put a muzzle on his face.

(ADVISERS *leave shaking fists at* KING D *and* DANIEL. *They return after* DANIEL *and* KING D *have left.)*

ADVISER 1: I hate Daniel.

ADVISER 2: I hate, duh, I hate Daniel too.

ADVISER 1: He's a slave, one of those Hebrews. I want to get rid of him.

ADVISER 2: Duh, I want to get rid of him too.

ADVISER 1: He's too smart for us. We can't outwit him.

ADVISER 2: Duh, we can't outwit him.

ADVISER 1: I know. His religion. He's always praying to that God of his. We'll get King Darius to make a law that nobody can pray to any god or any person but King Darius himself.

ADVISER 2: King Darius himself.

ADVISER 1: Will you quit copying me?

ADVISER 2: Will you quit copying me?

(They exit beating on each other.)

NARRATOR: And King Darius, not really knowing much better, signed the law that these evil advisers suggested.

(HERALD *enters with scroll.)*

HERALD: Hear ye! Hear ye! King Darius has proclaimed that for the next 30 days anyone who asks a favor or prays to any god or any person other than King Darius will be thrown to the lions. *(Exits)*

NARRATOR: Do you think that this law will stop Daniel from praying to God whom he loves? Well, here comes Daniel now. Let's see what happens.

(DANIEL *enters.*)

DANIEL: Lord, I trust in You alone. Keep me safe from the trap that has been set for me. I put myself in Your care.

(ADVISERS *enter.*)

ADVISER 1: Look.

ADVISER 2: Uh, duh, look.

ADVISERS: He's praying to his God. Let's get the king.

(They run off and then in with KING D.)

ADVISER 1: Look!

ADVISER 2: Uh, duh, look!

ADVISERS: He's praying to his God. Feed him to the lions.

KING D: Daniel, why have you disobeyed me?

DANIEL: To have obeyed you would have been to disobey my Lord.

KING D: I cannot go back on my word. Arrest him and, gulp, feed him to the lions.

NARRATOR: And they took Daniel to be eaten by the lions.

(Actors enter as lions. They growl at audience and look hungry.)

KING D: May your God, whom you worship, continually deliver you. I can't look.

(He turns away.)

DANIEL: Lord, my God, I have depended on You. Save me, and rescue me, or else I shall be torn to pieces.

(Just as the LIONS *are about to devour* DANIEL, *the* NARRATOR *speaks.)*

NARRATOR: And the Lord God sent an angel to shut the lions' mouths so they couldn't eat Daniel.

(LIONS *whimper, rub mouths with paws.*)

KING D: I can't bear to look. Will you kids tell me when Daniel has been eaten by the lions so we can take him out and give him a decent burial? *(Response from audience)* I can't stand the sight of blood. Is it a mess in there? *(Response)* Daniel, what's this? He's not dead. But how could this be?

DANIEL: You see, King Darius, the power of prayer and of love for my God?

KING D: I do see indeed. Throw them to the lions.
(ADVISERS *get chased out and eaten by the* LIONS.)
This is my latest decree. Listen, Daniel . . .

(HERALD *enters.*)

HERALD: Hear ye! Hear ye! I decree that everyone shall tremble and fear before the God of Daniel in every part of my kingdom. For his God is the living, unchanging God whose kingdom shall never be destroyed and whose power shall never end. He saves His people, preserving them from harm. He does great miracles in heaven and earth. It is He who saved Daniel from the power of the lions.

NARRATOR: Do you know that each one of you have been thrown to the lions? That's right, because sin is like those lions—it will tear you to pieces and hurt you. But just as God saved Daniel because Daniel put his trust in God alone, so will God save you if you put your trust in Jesus Christ. Yes, Jesus died so that we might be freed from sin. Our God is a saving God! Let's all sing the "Daniel Song" one more time. *(Exit)*

THE END